Who is Afraid of the Chinese Dragon? I Am

Who is Afraid of the Chinese Dragon? I Am

Col. Bhaskar Sarkar, VSM

PEACOCK BOOKS

Published by
PEACOCK BOOKS
7/22, Ansari Road, Darya Ganj,
New Delhi-110002
Phones : +91-11-40775252, 23273880, 23275880, 23280451
Fax : +91-11-23285873
Web : www.atlanticbooks.com
E-mail : orders@atlanticbooks.com

Branch Office
5, Nallathambi Street, Wallajah Road,
Chennai-600002
Phones : +91-44-64611085, 32413319
E-mail : chennai@atlanticbooks.com

Peacock Books is an imprint of
Atlantic Publishers and Distributors (P) Ltd

Printed in India at Nice Printing Press, A-33/3A, Site-IV,
Industrial Area, Sahibabad, Ghaziabad, U.P.

Dedication

This book is dedicated to the Indian soldiers whose lives were sacrificed by our gullible, unprofessional, self-seeking political and military leadership and bureaucrats, who sent them to defend our borders without proper weapons, equipment, clothing or infrastructure and to fight an unequal war with the Chinese in 1962, in the hope that 1962 is never repeated

Prologue

> The art of war teaches us not to rely on the likelihood of the enemy not coming but on our readiness to receive him; not on the chance of his not attacking but rather on the fact that we have made our position unassailable.
>
> —Sun Tzu, Chinese scholar and military strategist, in 500 BC

India is a soft state. Our patriotism is limited to dying for the country. It is noteworthy that some officers of the Mumbai police and the anti-terrorist squad, who were killed on 26/11 during the Mumbai terror attack, were awarded the highest gallantry awards, and not censured for incompetence and lack of tactical ability. Actually, we do not believe in preparing for war or winning wars. When Mohammad Ghori used to attack the Somnath Temple of Gujarat, thousands of Indians rushed to battle with whatever weapons they could muster and were massacred by Mohammad's well-trained and well-equipped forces. The invaders went away with gold, jewelry and women. They kept returning year after year and sacked the Somnath Temple no less than thirteen times without effective resistance. Things have not changed since then. We have fought four wars with Pakistan and won one in 1971. That victory was possible because the Army Chief of the time, General Sam Manekshaw, refused to attack East Pakistan till his forces were ready. We ran out of ammunition for Bofors guns and coffins during the Kargil war and had to resort to emergency purchases. Our soldiers still die at Siachin, Kashmir and in border skirmishes due to lack of proper equipment. Fighter pilots of the Air Force die in large numbers in peace time training due to old aircraft and poor maintenance. Politicians, people and media eulogize the sacrifices of the armed forces. Awards and grants of lands and petrol pumps are announced after wars, though not always released. Then everyone forgets the lessons of the war and it becomes business as usual. The intelligentsia and electronic media criticize the size of the defence budget. The armed forces and their requirements for modernization and maintenance are put on the back burner. Large parts of budget allocation for modernization remain unspent every year due to bureaucratic bungling. No one cares. Service Chiefs never complain lest their post-retirement benefits are endangered.

Our political leaders and administrators have an ostrich mentality. Pandit Nehru was either so gullible that he saw no danger in the induction of Chinese Army into Tibet or found it expedient to ignore it. There was no monitoring of Chinese activities in Aksai Chin area of Ladakh. Our government became aware of Chinese incursions only after the Chinese had annexed Aksai Chin. We paid no attention to modernizing our defence forces until after the 1962 debacle. We fought state-of-the-art American Patton tanks of the Pakistan Army during the 1965 War with Second World War Sherman and Centurion tanks. The Sherman tank shells used to bounce off the Patton tanks and could cause no damage. We survived the war without major losses due to some good fortune and inept strategic and tactical ability of the Pakistani Generals.

The demography of Assam is changing due to unchecked illegal immigration from Bangladesh. But our political leadership is unwilling to act due to vote bank politics. In fact, the figures are being hidden from the public domain. We allowed Pakistan to quietly occupy Kargil. We ignored the growth of the ULFA in Assam and the Naxalites in much of Bihar, Jharkhand, Orissa, Chhattisgarh and Maharashtra. Our Air Force still flies the accident prone MIG 21 known as "Flying Coffin". MIG 29 planes have been phased out by Russia but are frontline fighters of the Indian Air Force. Our cities have been targets of bomb blasts since 1993. I wonder if the terrorist attack in Mumbai on 26/11/2008 can wake up our political leaders from their slumber.

The armed forces have been relegated to the fringes of power and play second fiddle to the politicians, bureaucrats and even police officers. Essential equipments and spares are not procured in time. Pliable officers are promoted to positions of authority. National Security Guard (NSG), which is manned almost entirely by army officers and jawans, has an IPS officer to head the organization.

The future of our country depends not only on our economic policies but also on our defence and foreign policies. These in turn depend on the ability and acumen of our political leaders, security advisers, intellectuals and media to read the military capabilities and intentions of our neighbours. The year 1962 found the nation unprepared to meet the Chinese aggression. Unless we become aware of Chinese preparations and strategies, we will be found wanting when the time comes, in the same way as we were found wanting in 1962.

The aim of this book is to make the Indian leaders and the Indian public aware of the extent to which the Chinese have encircled India over the last thirty years and the comparative weakness of the Indian Armed Forces vis-à-vis what China and its allies can deploy against us if they choose to. In the process, I hope our leaders will realize the precarious state of our defence preparedness and take positive actions before it becomes too late.

It is not out of place to mention that all information related to military strengths of countries as well as economic data given in the book are based either on the Internet or published books. No access to classified information has been made. The book will be useful to policymakers, defence strategists and those working in military and paramilitary forces. The common readers and people from the media will find it highly informative.

Bhaskar Sarkar

Web: www.bhaskarsarkar.com
E-mail: bhaskar@bhaskarsarkar.com

Contents

Part 1
Background

Historical Relations

1

Background

Both India and China are large ancient nations whose history dates back almost 5000 years. There is a long history of trade and cultural exchanges between the two countries. But there were hardly any military conflicts between the two. This was perhaps due to the formidable Karakorum and Himalayan ranges which made large scale military expeditions unsustainable.

Sino-Sikh War

The Sino-Sikh War of 19th Century was one of the more recent conflicts. The Sikh Empire under Maharaja Ranjit Singh annexed Ladakh between 1834 and 1841. In 1841, the Sikh Army invaded Tibet and overran parts of western Tibet. Chinese forces regrouped and defeated the Sikh army in December 1841 and forced it to withdraw from Tibet. The Chinese forces then entered Ladakh and besieged Leh. They were in turn defeated by the Sikh Army. The Chinese and the Sikhs signed a treaty in September 1842 and agreed to respect the common borders. This treaty lays down the boundary between Ladakh and Tibet. The British defeated the Sikhs in 1846. This resulted in transfer of sovereignty over Ladakh to the British. However, both sides were apparently sufficiently satisfied that a traditional border was recognized and defined by natural elements and the border was not demarcated.

1857-1950

From 1857 to 1947, India was a British colony. During this period, the British did conduct a few campaigns in Tibet and signed some treaties with the government of Tibet regarding the boundaries between India and Tibet. It also accepted in principle that Tibet was a part of China. China saw considerable internal strife in early 20th Century which saw the end of the last Chinese Imperial Dynasty and rise of the republicans. This was followed by a civil war between the Nationalists and the Communists, Japanese occupation of the coastal regions, Second World War and finally another round of civil war. The Tibetans took advantage of this turmoil and declared themselves independent in 1912. They enjoyed this independence till 1949.

1950-1984

The "Peoples Republic of China (PRC)" was established on 1st April 1950. India was the 16th state to establish diplomatic relations with it. Mao Zedong, the Chairman of the Communist Party of China viewed Tibet as an integral part of the Chinese State. Mao was determined to bring Tibet under direct administrative and military control of PRC. It considered Indian concern over human rights violations in Tibet as an interference by the Indian Government in the internal affairs of the PRC. The PRC took control over Tibet and ended Dalai Lama's domination by force of arms in 1950. To avoid antagonizing China, Nehru informed Chinese leaders that India did not have any political or territorial ambitions in Tibet. With Indian support, Tibetan delegates signed an agreement in May 1951 recognizing PRC sovereignty but guaranteeing that the existing political and social system of Tibet would continue.

Nehru had dreamt of Sino-Indian friendship. He spelt out the "five principles of peaceful co-existence" between the two countries in the "Panchsheel Treaty" of 1954. The catch phrase of India's diplomacy with China in the 1950s was *Hindi-Chini bhai-bhai*, which means that Indians and Chinese are brothers. In 1954, India published new maps that included the Aksai Chin region within the boundaries of India. Then an Indian reconnaissance party discovered a completed Chinese road running through the Aksai Chin region. Border clashes and Indian protests became more frequent and serious. In

January 1959, PRC Premier Zhou En-lai wrote to Nehru rejecting Nehru's contention that the border was based on any existing treaty and custom and pointed out that no government in China had ever accepted the McMahon Line, which defined the eastern section of the border between India and Tibet as legal. China claimed 104,000 sq km of territory over which India's maps showed clear sovereignty and demanded "rectification" of the entire border. Zhou En-lai proposed that China would relinquish its claim to most of India's north-east in exchange for India's abandonment of its claim to Aksai Chin. The Indian government, constrained by domestic public opinion, rejected the idea of a settlement based on uncompensated loss of territory as being humiliating and unequal.

Relations between the two countries soured in 1959 when Tibetan spiritual leader Dalai Lama fled communist persecution and was given asylum in India with 15,000 of his followers. Soon after, the border dispute worsened between the two countries. China claimed Aksai Chin in the western sector and India claimed territories south of the McMahon Line in the eastern sector.

Some retired government servants have suggested that India failed to avail of a great opportunity of settling the border question at the time of Chinese Premier Zhou En-lai's visit to New Delhi in April 1960 when the Chinese were also keen to close the issue. They do not dwell on the fact that this could only have been achieved if India had ceded all the territories which China had quietly annexed in Ladakh between 1950 and 1960 and also Tawang. Sections of the Congress party along with Opposition MPs like Atal Behari Vajpayee opposed the move.

Border disputes resulted in a short border war between the People's Republic of China and India. The war started on 20th October 1962. Within a few weeks, the Chinese Army pushed the ill-prepared and inadequately led Indian forces to within forty-eight kilometers of the Assam plains, consolidated their hold on Aksai Chin and occupied strategic points in Ladakh. China declared a unilateral ceasefire on 21 November

1962 and withdrew twenty kilometres behind the actual line of control. Indians believe that India was attacked by China in 1962. However, Neville Maxwell in his book *India's China War* held India primarily responsible for the border war. Indian authorities have never accepted this in public, although privately his views have considerable support amongst Indian scholars and experts.

Relations between the PRC and India deteriorated during the rest of the 1960s and the early 1970s. China diplomatically backed Pakistan in its 1965 war with India. Between 1967 and 1971, an all weather road was built in Pakistan Occupied Kashmir (POK) linking China's Xinjiang Province with Pakistan. India could do no more than protest. China supplied ideological, financial and other assistance to dissident groups, especially to Naga insurgents in north-eastern India. China also accused India of assisting the Khampa rebels in Tibet. Diplomatic contact between the two governments was minimal although not formally severed. Border clashes continued to occur. In late 1967, there were two skirmishes between Indian and Chinese forces in Sikkim. The first one was dubbed the "Nathu La incident", and the other the "Cho La incident".

On 11th September 1967, troops of the Indian Army's 18th Rajput Regiment were protecting an Engineering Company that was fencing the border at Nathu La when Chinese troops opened fire on them. This escalated over the next five days to an exchange of heavy artillery and mortar fire between the Indians and the Chinese. 62 Indian soldiers, from the 18th Rajput, the 2nd Grenadiers and the Artillery regiments were killed. Major Harbhajan Singh of the Rajput Regiment was awarded a Mahavir Chakra (posthumous) and Naib Subedar Pandey a Vir Chakra (posthumous) for their gallant actions. The extent of Chinese casualties in this incident is not known.

On 1 October 1967, a group of Indian soldiers noticed Chinese troops surrounding a sentry post at the Cho La outpost on Sikkim Tibet border. After a heated argument over the control of the area, a Chinese soldier bayoneted a Gurkha rifleman, triggering the start of a close quarters knife and fire fight, which then escalated to a mortar and heavy machine gun duel. The Chinese troops signalled a ceasefire after three hours of fighting but later scaled Point 15450 to establish themselves there. The Gurkhas outflanked them the next day to regain Point 15450 and the Chinese retreated across the Line of Actual Control (LAC). 21 Indian soldiers were killed in this action. The Indian government awarded Vir Chakras to Rifleman Limbu (posthumous) and battalion commander Major K.B. Joshi for their gallant actions. The extent of Chinese casualties in this skirmish is also not known.

India and China renewed efforts to improve relations after 1979. China remained silent on India's annexation of Sikkim and its special relationship with Bhutan. The Chinese leaders agreed to discuss the boundary issue. Mount Kailash and Mansarovar Lake in Tibet were opened to annual pilgrimages from India. In 1980, Indian Prime Minister Indira Gandhi approved a plan to upgrade the deployment of forces around the Line of Actual Control to avoid unilateral redefinitions of the line. India also increased funds for infrastructure development in these areas. In 1981, the Chinese minister of foreign affairs was invited to India.

1984-1996

In 1984, squads of Indian soldiers began actively patrolling the Sumdorong Chu Valley in Arunachal Pradesh. The area was claimed by both sides. The Indian team had left the area before the winter. In the winter of 1986, the Chinese deployed their troops to the Sumdorong Chu before the Indian troops could arrive in the summer and built a helipad at Wandung. Surprised by the Chinese occupation, Indian Army airlifted a brigade to the region. Chinese troops could not move any further into the valley and were forced to move sideways along the Thag La ridge, away from the valley. By 1987, Beijing's reaction was similar to that in 1962 and this prompted many Western diplomats to predict war. However, Indian foreign minister and Prime Minister travelled to Beijing in 1988 and negotiated a mutual de-escalation.

India and China held eight rounds of border negotiations between December 1981 and November 1987. These talks initially raised hopes that progress could be made on the border issue. However, in 1985 the Chinese stiffened their position on the border and wanted concessions without defining the exact terms of its "package proposal" or where the Line of Actual Control (LAC) lay. India granted statehood to Arunachal Pradesh in February 1987. This caused both sides to deploy new troops to the area, raising tensions and fears of a new border war. The PRC relayed warnings that it would "teach India a lesson" if it did not cease "nibbling" at Chinese territory. By the summer of 1987, however, both sides had backed away from conflict and denied that military clashes had taken place.

1988-2003

Improvement in relations between the two countries was facilitated by Rajeev Gandhi's visit to China in December 1988. It was the first visit by an Indian Prime Minister to China since Nehru's 1954 visit. The two sides issued a joint communique that stressed the need to restore friendly relations on the basis of the principles of "Panchsheel". India and the People's Republic of China agreed to broaden bilateral ties in various areas and work to achieve a "fair and reasonable settlement while seeking a mutually acceptable solution" to the border dispute. The communique also expressed China's concern about agitation by Tibetan separatists in India and reiterated China's position that Tibet was an integral part of China. Rajeev Gandhi signed bilateral agreements on cooperation in science and technology, on civil aviation to establish direct air links and on cultural exchanges. The two sides also agreed to hold annual diplomatic consultations between foreign ministers and to set up a joint ministerial committee on economic and scientific cooperation and a joint working group on the boundary issue. The latter group was to be led by the Indian foreign secretary and the Chinese Vice minister of foreign affairs.

The mid-1990s showed a slow but steady improvement in relations with China. Top level dialog continued with the December 1991 visit of Chinese Premier Li Peng to India and the May 1992 visit to China of Indian President R. Venkataraman. Progress was also made in reducing tensions on the border via confidence-building measures, including mutual troop reductions, regular meetings of local military commanders and advance notification of military exercises. Border trade resumed in July 1992 after a gap of more than thirty years. Consulates reopened in Mumbai and Shanghai in 1992. The two sides agreed to open an additional border trading post in 1993.

Prime Minister Narsimha Rao and Premier Li Peng signed the border agreement and three other agreements on cross-border trade, on increased cooperation on environment and in radio and television broadcasting during the former's visit to Beijing in September 1993. A senior level Chinese military delegation made a six-day goodwill visit to India in December 1993. India ignored reports that China was exporting large amounts of military material to Burma's army, navy and air force and sending an increasing number of technicians to Burma. Indian authorities also played down the presence of Chinese radar technicians in Burma's Coco Islands, which border the Andaman and Nicobar Islands. The 1993 Chinese military delegation's visit to India was reciprocated by Indian army chief of staff in 1994. The border issue was raised in September 1994, when Chinese Defence Minister visited New Delhi for extensive talks with high-level Indian trade and defence officials. Further talks were held in New Delhi in March 1995, by the India-China Expert Group. The two sides were reported to be "seriously engaged" in defining the McMahon Line and the LAC. In January 1994, Beijing announced that it not only favoured a negotiated solution on the Kashmir Issue but also opposed any form of independence for the region. Mr. George Fernandes, then Defence Minister visited China in 1996. Zhang Zemin, the Chairman of the Central Military Commission in 1996, greeted Mr. Fernandes in an unprecedented gesture. In December 1996, President Jhang Zemin most unexpectedly told his Pakistani hosts that India and Pakistan must set aside their differences and foster an economic relationship. During the Kargil war, the Chinese stance was a tacit acceptance of the LOC in Jammu and Kashmir as the international border.

India-China relations nosedived again in May 1998, after India conducted nuclear tests. Some believe that Mr. Vajpayee as Prime Minister wrote to President Bill Clinton pointing to China as the reason for India going nuclear. Mr. George Fernandes was widely quoted as having said that China is India's enemy number one. But he consistently denied ever having made such a statement. India also accused China of supporting Pakistan's nuclear and missile programs. Relations between India and China stayed strained until the end of the decade.

Indian President K.R. Narayana visited China in 2000. This marked a gradual diplomatic re-engagement of India and China. In a major embarrassment for China, the 17th Karamapa, Urggyen Trinley Dorje, who was proclaimed by China, made a dramatic escape from Tibet to the Rumtak Monastery in Sikkim. Chinese officials were in a quandary on this issue as any protest to India on the issue would mean an explicit endorsement on India's governance of Sikkim, which the Chinese still hadn't recognized. In 2002, Chinese Premier Zhu Rongji reciprocated the President's visit by visiting India with a focus on economic issues. The year 2003 ushered in a marked improvement in Sino-Indian relations following Indian Prime Minister Atal Bihari Vajpayee's visit to China in June 2003. China officially recognized Indian sovereignty over Sikkim as the two nations moved toward resolving their border disputes.

2004-2008

The year 2004 also witnessed a gradual improvement in relations. The Nathu La and Jelep La passes in Sikkim were opened for border trade. The year 2004 was a milestone in Sino-Indian bilateral trade which surpassed the $10 billion mark for the first time. In April 2005, Chinese Premier Wen Jiabao visited Bangalore to push for increased Sino-Indian cooperation in high-tech industries. The high level visit produced several agreements to deepen political, cultural and economic ties between the two nations. But China has not supported India on the issue of India gaining a permanent seat on the UN Security Council. China was granted an observer status in the SAARC Summit of 2005. While other countries in the region are ready to consider China for permanent membership in the SAARC, India is reluctant.

In November 2006, China and India had a verbal spat over claim of the north-eastern Indian state of Arunachal Pradesh. India claimed that China was occupying 38,000 sq km of its territory in Kashmir, while China claimed the whole of Arunachal Pradesh as its own. In May 2007, China denied the application for visa from an IAS officer from Arunachal Pradesh. According to China, since Arunachal Pradesh is a territory of China, he did not need a visa to visit his own country. Later in December 2007, China appeared to have reversed its policy by granting the visa to Marpe Sora, an Arunachal born professor in computer science. In January 2008, Prime Minister Manmohan Singh visited China and met with President Hu Jintao and Premier Wen Jiabao and had bilateral discussions related to trade, commerce, defence, military and various other issues.

A very important dimension of the evolving Sino-Indian relationship is their cooperations in Doha Round of negotiations with developed nations on WTO. A degree of cooperation is visible, as they are increasingly confronting bigger players in the global market. The British Government recognized Chinese sovereignty over Tibet in 2008 by issuing a statement on its website.

On January 14, 2008, during his first official visit to Beijing, Indian Prime Minister Manmohan Singh sat down with Chinese Premier Wen Jiabao in the Great Hall of the People to emphasize what the two Asian giants have in common. The leaders signed a seven-page document that covers issues such as their fast-growing economic ties, defence cooperation, anti-terrorism efforts, climate change and energy policies. Noting that India and China "are the two largest developing nations on earth representing more than one-third of humanity," the document goes on to note that the countries with a history of mutual suspicion are now "convinced that it is time to look to the future in building a relationship," and that "China-India friendship and common development will have a positive influence on the future of the world."

Conclusion

Historical relations between India and China have been largely restricted to trade and cultural exchanges. But post

1950, their relations have been plagued by border disputes, Tibet and regional rivalry. Both sides are trying to improve relations and down play differences. India and China held their first joint military training exercise in the Chinese city of Kumming which is in Yunnan Province bordering Arunachal. Only time will tell whether the mutual rivalry and historical problems or pragmatism will prevail.

Conflicts of Interest

2

Introduction

There are some issues between the two countries which are difficult to resolve. The first and most pressing problem is the territorial dispute. Both neighbours claim that the other occupies territory that is rightfully theirs. The second insolvable problem is the presence of Dalai Lama and Tibetan refugees in India. China sees these people as a potential threat to its hold over Tibet. It is impossible for India to deport Dalai Lama and the Tibetan refugees to Tibet. There are other problems too. India cannot ignore of China's military alliances with Pakistan, Bangladesh, Sri Lanka, Burma and Nepal. This aspect is discussed in detail in Part 2 of this book.

China has its own worries. It was none too pleased with the so-called axis of democracy created by President George Bush that included India, Japan, Australia and the United States. Beijing believes the close cooperation between these four countries was directed against China. However, the axis has collapsed with change of government in Australia and arrival of Barack Obama as the new US President. Still, India's growing closeness to the U.S., including the India-U.S. nuclear cooperation, has China nervous.

The Border Dispute

Aksai Chin

As explained in Chapter 1, the Chinese and the Sikhs signed a treaty in September 1842, which laid down the boundary between Ladakh and Tibet. The sovereignty of Ladakh was transferred to the British when they defeated the

Sikhs in 1846. The border was defined by natural features and never demarcated. The points at the two extremities of the disputed boundary in Kashmir, Pangong Lake (Pso) and Karakorum Pass, were well defined, but the Aksai Chin area which lay in between these two features lay undefined. W.H. Johnson, an officer with the Survey of India, proposed the "Johnson Line" as border between Ladakh and Tibet in 1865. This line puts Aksai Chin in Kashmir. This line was never presented to the Chinese for ratification. Johnson presented this line to the Maharaja of Kashmir, who then claimed the 38,000 sq km territory. By 1892, China had erected border trading posts at Karakorum Pass and Khunjareb Pass. At this time, Britain and China were allies and Britain was principally concerned that Aksai Chin does not fall into Russian hands. When China showed an interest in Aksai Chin, Britain proposed a revised boundary, called the McCartney-Macdonald Line, which puts most of Aksai Chin in Chinese territory. This line ran along the Karakorum Mountains. The Karakorum Mountains formed a natural boundary up to the Indus River watershed. It left the Tarim River basin in Chinese control. In 1899, the British presented this line to the Chinese, who raised no objection to it. This line is approximately the same as the current Line of Actual Control. Both lines were used on British maps of India. Central power in China collapsed in 1911 with the collapse of the Manchu Qing Dynasty and Tibet declared independence. At the end of World War I, the British officially used the Johnson Line in their maps. But they took no steps to establish outposts or assert actual control on the ground. In 1927, the border was adjusted again as the British Government in India abandoned the Johnson line in favour of the McCartney-Macdonald Line along the Karakorum range further south. However, the maps were not updated and still showed the Johnson Line. The boundary remained undemarcated at India's independence. After independence in 1947, the Indian government used the Johnson Line as the basis for its official boundary in the west. Thus, the Aksai Chin area became a part of India on its maps. In July 1954, Prime Minister Nehru directed that the maps of India be revised to show definite boundaries on all frontiers. Up to this point, the boundary in the Aksai Chin sector, based on the Johnson Line, had been described as "undemarcated". During the 1950s, China built a 1,200 km road connecting Xinjiang Province and western Tibet. Of this, 179 km ran south of the Johnson Line through the Aksai Chin region claimed by India. Aksai Chin was easily accessible to the Chinese, but was more difficult for the Indians on the other side of the Karakorum to reach. The Indians did not learn of the existence of the road until 1957. The road was confirmed when it was shown in Chinese maps published in 1958. In October 13, 1962, China and Pakistan began negotiations over the boundary west of the Karakorum Pass and in 1963, the two countries settled their boundaries largely on the basis of the McCartney-Macdonald Line.

The Indian position, as stated by Prime Minister Jawaharlal Nehru was that the Aksai Chin was "part of the Ladakh region of India for centuries" and that this northern border was a "firm and definite one which was not open to discussion with anybody". The Chinese Prime Minister, Zhou En-lai argued that the western border had never been demarcated, that the McCartney-Macdonald Line, which left the Aksai Chin within Chinese borders was the only line ever proposed to a Chinese government and that the Aksai Chin was already under Chinese jurisdiction and that negotiations should take into account the status quo.

McMahon Line

The British annexed Assam and the north eastern states by the Treaty of Yandaboo at the conclusion of the First Anglo Burmese War in 1826. This resulted in India and China having a common border other than India's border with Tibet. In 1913-14, representatives of Britain, China, and Tibet attended a conference in Shimla, India and drew up an agreement concerning Tibet's status and borders. The McMahon Line, a proposed boundary between Tibet, China and India for the eastern sector, was drawn by British negotiator Henry McMahon on a map attached to the agreement. All three representatives initialed the agreement, but Beijing immediately objected to the proposed Sino-Tibet boundary and repudiated the agreement. Some reports suggest that McMahon had been instructed not to sign the treaty bilaterally with Tibetans if

China refused, but he did so without the Chinese representative present and then kept the declaration secret. China claims that by signing the Shimla Agreement with Tibet, the British had violated the Anglo-Chinese Convention of 1906, which bound the British government "not to annex Tibetan territory." Because of doubts concerning the legal status of the accord, the British did not put the McMahon Line on their maps until 1937, nor did they publish the Shimla Convention in the treaty record until 1938. Indian government held the view that the Himalayas were the ancient boundaries of the Indian sub-continent and thus should be the boundaries of British India and later independent India.

China argued that the Shimla Convention and McMahon Line were illegal and that Tibet was not an independent country in 1913 and did not have any treaty making powers. Tibetan officials continued to administer Tawang and refused to concede the territory during negotiations in 1938. The situation remained the same till the British annexed Tawang region during World War II. In 1947, Tibet requested that India recognize Tibetan authority over Tawang, south of the McMahon Line. This was rejected.

China's claim on areas south of the McMahon Line, encompassing Arunachal Pradesh, were based on traditional boundaries between India and Tibet. India believes that the boundaries China proposed in Ladakh and Arunachal Pradesh have no written basis and no documentation of acceptance by anyone apart from China. Indians argue that China claims the territory on the basis that it was under Chinese imperial control in the past, while Chinese argue that India claims the territory on the basis that it was under British imperial control in the past. India claims that the intent of the treaty of 1913 was to follow the highest ridges of the Himalayas while demarcating the border. They claimed that South of the highest ridges should be Indian territory and North of the highest ridges should be Chinese territory. In the Indian claim, the two armies would be separated from each other by the highest mountains in the world. Parts of India's claim line in the eastern sector follow a modified version of the McMahon Line. The original line drawn up by Henry McMahon on the Shimla

Treaty map starts at 27°44'30"N, starting a tri-junction between Bhutan, China and India and from there, extends eastwards. Starting from the 1950s, when India began patrolling this area, they found that they at multiple locations, the highest ridges fell north of the McMahon Line as shown in the treaty map and their own maps and they modified their maps to extend the boundary northwards to include features such as Thag La, Longju, and Khinzemane as Indian territories. Thus, the Indian version of the McMahon Line moves the Bhutan-China-India tri-junction north to 27°48'N. India claims that the treaty map ran along features such as Thag La, though the actual treaty map itself is topographically vague (as the treaty was not accompanied with demarcation). The treaty includes no verbal description of geographic features nor description of the highest ridges.

Presence of Dalai Lama and Tibetan Refugees in India

Early History of Sino-Tibetan Relations

The first known interaction between China and Tibet was in 640 A.D., when the Tibetan King Songtsan Gampo married the niece of the Tang Emperor Taizong. Gampo's descendants conquered the vast region that now forms the Chinese provinces of Qinghai, Gansu and Xinjiang (often referred to as inner Tibet) between 663 and 692. In 692, the Chinese retook Inner Tibet. The Tibetan king then allied himself with the Arabs and eastern Turks. Chinese Imperial forces under General Gao Xianzhi conquered Tibet and much of Central Asia, until he was defeated by the Arabs and Turks at the battle of Talas River in 751. The Chinese withdrew and Tibet regained control of much of Xinjiang and Inner Tibet. Tibetans even seized the Tang Chinese capital city of Changan (now Xian) in 763. Tibet and China signed a peace treaty in 821 or 822, which delineated the border between the two empires. Status quo was maintained till the rise of the Mongols under Genghis Khan who conquered China and Tibet. Tibet came to be considered one of the thirteen provinces of Mongol Yuan Dynasty. The Mongols' Yuan Empire fell in 1368 to the Han Chinese Ming Dynasty. Tibet reasserted its independence and refused to pay tribute to the new Emperor.

Origin of Dalai Lama

In 1474, the Lama of an important Tibetan Buddhist monastery, Gendun Drup, passed away. A child born two years later was found to be a reincarnation of the Lama and was raised to be the next leader of that sect, Gendun Gyatso. After their lifetimes, the two men were called the First and Second Dalai Lama. Their sect, the Gelug or "Yellow Hats", became the dominating sect of Tibetan Buddhism. The Third Dalai Lama, Sonam Gyatso (1543-88) was responsible for converting the Mongols to Gelug Tibetan Buddhism. The Mongol ruler Altan Khan was a follower of the Dalai Lama. The Gtsang-pa Dynasty assumed the royal throne of Tibet in 1562 and ruled Tibet for the next 80 years. The Fourth Dalai Lama, Yonten Gyatso (1589-1616), was a Mongolian prince and the grandson of Altan Khan.

During the 1630s, China was embroiled in power struggles between the Mongols, Han Chinese of the fading Ming Dynasty and the Manchu people of north-eastern China (Manchuria) and were unable to dominate Tibet. The Manchus eventually defeated the Han in 1644 and established China's last imperial dynasty, the Qing Dynasty (1644-1912).

Tibet saw a power struggle between Kagyu (Red Hats) Tibetan Buddhists and the Yellow Hats in 1634. The great general Gushi Khan, of the Oirad Mongols supported the Yellow Hats who prevailed. The Fifth Dalai Lama, Lobsang Gyatso, became the spiritual and temporal head over all of Tibet in 1642 with Mongol help. The Potala Palace in Lhasa was constructed as a symbol of this new synthesis of secular and temporal power. The Dalai Lama made a state visit to the Qing Dynasty's second Emperor, Shunzhi, in 1653. The Dalai Lama was recognized as the spiritual authority of the Qing Empire. The fifth Dalai Lama died in 1682. This was followed by a succession struggle. The Sixth Dalai Lama was finally enthroned in 1697. His unconventional lifestyle prompted Lobsang Khan of the Khoshud Mongols to depose him in 1705. Lobsang Khan seized control of Tibet, named himself King and appointed a pretender Dalai Lama. Lobsang Khan ruled for 12 years until the Dzungar Mongols invaded and took power. They killed the pretender to the Dalai Lama's throne. This was appreciated by the Tibetan people. But the Mongols then began to loot monasteries around Lhasa. This vandalism brought a quick response from the Qing Emperor Kangxi, who sent Chinese troops into Tibet. The Dzungars defeated the Imperial Chinese army near Lhasa in 1718. In 1720, Emperor Kangxi sent another, larger force to Tibet, which crushed the Dzungars. The Qing army also brought the proper Seventh Dalai Lama, Kelzang Gyatso (1708-57) to Lhasa and installed him as the ruler of Tibet. China took advantage of this period of instability in Tibet to seize the regions of Amdo and Kham, including them into the Chinese province of Qinghai in 1724. However, the area was ruled through Tibetan nobles. Three years later, the Chinese and Tibetans signed a treaty that laid out the boundary line between the two nations which remained in force until 1910.

In 1788, the Regent of Nepal sent a Gurkha forces to invade Tibet. The Qing Emperor responded in strength and the Nepalese retreated. The Gurkhas returned three years later, plundering and destroying some famous Tibetan monasteries. The Chinese sent a force of 17,000 which, along with Tibetan troops, drove the Gurkhas out of Tibet to within 30 km of Kathmandu. Despite this sort of assistance from the Chinese Empire, the people of Tibet chafed under increasingly meddlesome Qing rule.

Between 1804, when the Eighth Dalai Lama died, and 1895, when the Thirteenth Dalai Lama assumed the throne, none of the incumbent incarnations of the Dalai Lama lived to see their nineteenth birthdays. If the Chinese found a certain incarnation too hard to control, they would poison him. If the Tibetans thought an incarnation was controlled by the Chinese, then they would poison him themselves.

British Influence

Russia and Britain were engaged in a struggle for influence and control in Central Asia. Tibet was an important player in this game. In 1893, the British in India concluded a trade and border treaty with Beijing concerning the boundary between Sikkim and Tibet. However, the Tibetans flatly rejected the treaty terms. The British invaded Tibet in 1903 and took Lhasa the following year. When the British mission reached Lhasa, the Dalai Lama had already fled to Mongolia. So, the leader of the expedition, Younghusband, drafted a treaty unilaterally and had it signed at the Potala Palace by the Regent Lama, Ganden Tri Rinpoche, and other Tibetan officials. The Anglo-Tibetan treaty was confirmed by a Sino-British treaty in 1906 by which the Government of Great Britain agreed not to annex Tibetan territory or to interfere in the administration of Tibet. The Government of China also undertook not to permit any other foreign State to interfere with the territory or internal administration of Tibet. Beijing also agreed to pay London 2.5 million rupees which Lhasa was forced to agree upon in the Anglo-Tibetan treaty of 1904. In 1907, Britain and Russia accepted the suzerainty of China over Tibet and agreed not to negotiate with Tibet except through the intermediary of the Chinese Government.

The 13th Dalai Lama had fled Tibet in 1904 in the face of British attack on Lhasa. The Chinese declared that the Dalai Lama had been deposed as soon as he left Tibet and claimed full sovereignty over not only Tibet but also Nepal and Bhutan. The Dalai Lama went to Beijing to discuss the situation with the Qing Emperor Guangxu. He stayed in the Chinese capital from 1906 to 1908.

Qing Dynasty Reclaims Tibet 1905-1912

The Qing government appointed Zhao Erfeng, the Governor of Xinjiang, "Army Commander of Tibet" to reintegrate Tibet into China. He reached Tibet in 1905 on a punitive expedition. His troops destroyed a number of monasteries in Kham and Amdo. He abolished the powers of the Tibetan nobles and appointed Chinese magistrates in their places. He introduced new laws that limited the number of Lamas at a monastery and deprived monasteries of their temporal power. He started schemes for having the land cultivated by Chinese immigrants. Zhao's methods in northern Tibet were uncannily similar to those adopted by the Communists nearly half a century later. They were aimed at the extermination of the Tibetan clergy, the assimilation of territory and re-population of the Tibetan plateaus with poor peasants from China. Like the later Chinese conquerors,

Zhao's men looted and destroyed Tibetan monasteries, melted down religious images and tore up sacred texts. Zhao Erfeng worked out a comprehensive scheme for the redevelopment of Tibet that covered military training, reclamation work, secular education, trade and administration. After the Qing government was confident that their control over Tibet had been sufficiently consolidated, the Dalai Lama's title's was restored in November 1908, and he was about to return to Lhasa from Amdo in the summer of 1909. The Chinese decided to send military forces to Lhasa to keep control over him. The Dalai Lama once again fled, this time to India and was once again deposed by the Chinese. The situation soon changed. After the fall of the Qing dynasty in October 1911, Zhao's Tibetan soldiers mutinied and beheaded him. The Dalai Lama returned to Tibet in 1912 and became its temporal and secular ruler.

Tibet Enjoys Independence (1912 to 1949)

By 1911, China was in turmoil and unable to intervene in Tibet. Japan invaded Manchuria in 1910 and occupied most of Chinese coastal regions up to 1945. The new government of the Republic of China held nominal power over the majority of Chinese territory for only four years before war broke out between numerous armed factions. China saw near continuous civil war up to the Communist victory in 1949.

In 1912, China's new revolutionary government issued a formal apology to the Dalai Lama for the Qing Dynasty's insults and offered to reinstate him as the spiritual leader. The Dalai Lama refused. He then issued a proclamation that was distributed across Tibet, rejecting Chinese control and stating that "We are a small, religious and independent nation". The Dalai Lama took control of Tibet's internal and external governance in 1913. He negotiated directly with foreign powers and reformed Tibet's judicial, penal and educational systems.

Representatives of Great Britain, China and Tibet met in 1914 to negotiate a treaty marking out the boundary lines between India and its northern neighbors. It was called the Shimla Convention of 1914. It granted China secular control over "Inner Tibet", while recognizing the autonomy of "Outer Tibet" under the Dalai Lama's rule. Both China and Britain promised to respect the territorial integrity of Tibet and to abstain from interference in the administration of Outer Tibet. China walked out of the conference without signing the treaty after Britain laid claim to the Tawang area of southern Tibet. Tibet and Britain signed the treaty.

The 13th Dalai Lama ruled independent Tibet in peace until his death in 1933. Following his death, the new reincarnation of the Dalai Lama was born in Amdo in 1935. Tenzin Gyatso, the 14th and current Dalai Lama, was taken to Lhasa in 1937 to begin training for his duties as the leader of Tibet. He remained there until 1959 when he fled to India.

The Chinese Take Over Tibet

In October 1950, the PLA invaded the Tibetan area of Chamdo and defeated sporadic resistance from the Tibetan army. In 1951, representatives of Tibetan authority, with Dalai Lama's authorization, participated in negotiations in Beijing with Chinese government. It resulted in a Seventeen Point Agreement which affirmed China's sovereignty over Tibet. The agreement was ratified in Lhasa a few months later. From the beginning, it was obvious that incorporating Tibet into Communist China would bring two opposite social systems face to face. In Tibet, the Chinese Communists opted not to place liberating the serfs as an immediate priority. From 1951 to 1959, traditional Tibetan society with its lords and manorial estates continued to function unchanged. Despite the presence of twenty thousand PLA troops in Central Tibet, the Dalai Lama's government was permitted to maintain important symbols from its de facto independence period.

The Chinese built highways that reached Lhasa. The road network was then extended to the Indian, Nepalese and Pakistani borders. Communists tried to establish rural communes in Inner Tibet, as was happening in the whole of China. Landholdings of the monasteries and nobility were seized for redistribution to the peasants. The communist forces hoped to destroy the power base of the wealthy and the Lama's within Tibetan society. By 1956, there was unrest in eastern

Kham and Amdo, where land reform had been implemented in full. These rebellions eventually spread into Outer Tibet. The uprising was led by the monks and continued till 1969. Initially, the rebels had considerable success with CIA support and aid. Some parts of southern Tibet fell into rebel control. The poorly armed Tibetans used guerrilla tactics in an attempt to drive out the Chinese. The PLA responded by razing entire villages and monasteries to the ground. The Chinese even threatened to blow up the Potala Palace and kill the Dalai Lama, but this threat was not carried out. According to the Dalai Lama's government in exile, the bitter fighting left an estimated 86,000 Tibetans dead. In 1959, China's military crackdown on rebels in Kham and Amdo led to the "Lhasa Uprising". Full scale resistance spread throughout Tibet. Fearing capture of the Dalai Lama, unarmed Tibetans surrounded his residence. Tibetan troops were able to secure a route for the Dalai Lama to escape into India on March 17. Actual fighting began on March 19 and lasted only two days before the Tibetan troops were defeated. Much of Lhasa lay in ruins by March 20, 1959. An estimated 800 artillery shells had pummeled Norbulingka. Three of Lhasa's largest monasteries were essentially leveled. The Chinese rounded up thousands of monks and executed many of them. Monasteries and temples all over Lhasa were ransacked. The remaining members of the Dalai Lama's bodyguard were publicly executed by firing squad. By the time of the 1964 census, 300,000 Tibetans had gone "missing" in the previous five years, either secretly imprisoned, killed or in exile. In the days after the 1959 Uprising, the Chinese government revoked most aspects of Tibet's autonomy, and initiated resettlement and land distribution across the country. Following the Lhasa uprising and the Dalai Lama's flight from Tibet in 1959, the government of India was politically pressured by Britain and US to accept the Tibetan refugees. The Tibetan resistance forces withdrew into areas bordering Nepal and continued operations. In 1969, on the eve of Kissenger's overtures to China, American support to the rebels was withdrawn and the Nepalese government dismantled the Tibetan resistance bases in Nepal.

In 1965, the area that had been under the control of the Dalai Lama's government from the 1910s to 1959 (Outer Tibet) was renamed the Tibet Autonomus Region or TAR. Autonomy provided that head of government would be an ethnic Tibetan. However, de facto power in the TAR is held by the general secretary of the Communist Party, who has always been a Han Chinese from outside of Tibet. The role of ethnic Tibetans in the higher levels of the TAR Communist Party remains limited. During the mid-1960s, the monastic estates were broken up and secular education introduced. During the Cultural Revolution in China, considerable damage was done to monasteries in Tibet. Thousands of Buddhist monks and nuns were killed, tortured or imprisoned. Since 1979, there have been economic reforms. Most religious freedoms have been officially restored, provided the Lama's accept Chinese rule, renounce the Dalai Lama and stay within dictated confines of their monasteries. Foreigners can visit most parts of Tibet, but it is claimed that the less savory aspects of Chinese rule are kept hidden from visitors.

Tibetans in Exile in India

The community of Tibetans in exile established in Dharamsala (Himachal Pradesh) and Karnataka, South India, has expanded since 1959. Tibetans have duplicated Tibetan monasteries in India and now house tens of thousands of monks. They have also created Tibetan schools, hospitals and established the Library of Tibetan Works and Archives, all aimed at continuing Tibetan tradition and culture. Tibetan festivals such as Lama dances, celebration of Losar, the Tibetan New Year, and the Monlam continue in exile. The plight of the Tibetan refugees garnered international attention when the Dalai Lama, spiritual and religious leader of the Tibetan government in exile, won the Nobel Peace Prize in 1989. The Dalai Lama was awarded the Nobel Prize on the basis of his unswerving commitment to peaceful protest against the Chinese occupation of Tibet. Among the most recent ceremonies and awards, he was given the Congressional Gold Medal by President Bush in 2007 and in 2006, he was one of only three people to ever receive an honorary Canadian citizenship. The Chinese consistently protested each official contact with the exiled Tibetan leader by western countries and their leaders.

China's central government, in a bid to dilute the Tibetan population, initiated a "Western China Development Program" in 1978. As many as 300,000 Han Chinese now live in Tibet, two-thirds of them in Lhasa. The Tibetan population of Lhasa, in contrast, is only 100,000. Ethnic Chinese hold the vast majority of government posts. In an attempt to gain acceptance, Beijing allowed the 10th Panchen Lama, Tibetan Buddhism's second-in-command, to return to Tibet in 1989. He died five days later at the age of 50, allegedly of a massive heart attack. China has made every effort to maintain a strangle hold on Tibet. Strict censorship is maintained. But occasionally, news of agitations by Tibetans and reports of human rights violations reach the outside world. One such incident was the deaths at Drapchi Prison in 1998 where Tibetan criminal and political detainees were brutalized for shouting anti-Chinese and pro-Dalai Lama slogans during a flag raising ceremony. Five nuns, three monks and one male criminal were reportedly killed by the guards.

In 1991, Dalai Lama stated that Chinese settlers in Tibet were creating "Chinese Apartheid". He alleged that the Chinese authorities were denying Tibetans, equal social and economic status in their own land. In 1995, the Dalai Lama named Gedhum Choekyi Nyima as the 11th Panchen Lama, while the Chinese named another child, Gyancain Norbu. Gyancain Norbu was raised in Beijing and has appeared occasionally on state media. The whereabouts of Gedhun Choekyi Nyima and his family are unknown. Amnesty International claims that they are imprisoned, while Beijing contends that they are living under a secret identity for protection and privacy.

In 2005, Chinese Premier Wen Jiabao offered to hold talks with the 14th Dalai Lama on the Tibet issue, provided he dropped the demand for independence. The Dalai Lama said in an interview with the *South China Morning Post* "We are willing to be part of the People's Republic of China, to have it govern and guarantee to preserve our Tibetan culture, spirituality and our environment." He had already said he would accept Chinese sovereignty over Tibet but insisted on real autonomy over its religious and cultural life. The Tibetan government in exile called on the Chinese government to respond. The move was seen to be unpopular with some Tibetans in exile, particularly among the younger generation. In January 2007, the Dalai Lama, in an interview on a private television channel, said "What we demand from the Chinese authority is more autonomy for Tibetans to protect their culture." He added that he had told the Tibetan people not to think in terms of history and to accept Tibet as a part of China.

On March 10, 2008, Tibetans marked the 49th anniversary of the 1959 uprising by peacefully protesting for the release of imprisoned monks and nuns. Chinese police broke up the protest with tear gas and gunfire. The protests continued for several more days and finally turned into a riot. Furious Tibetans ransacked and burned the shops of Han Chinese immigrants in Lhasa and other cities. The official Chinese media claimed that 18 people were killed by the rioters. China immediately cut off access to Tibet for foreign media and tourists. The unrest spread to neighbouring Qinghai (Inner Tibet), Gansu, and Sichuan Provinces. The Chinese government cracked down hard and mobilized about 50,000 troops. Reports indicate that the military killed between 80 and 140 people and arrested more than 2,300 Tibetans. The unrest came at a sensitive time for China, which was gearing up for the 2008 Summer Olympics in Beijing. The situation in Tibet caused increased international scrutiny of Beijing's entire human rights record, leading some foreign leaders to boycott the Olympic Opening Ceremonies. The same year, the Chinese government launched a 570 million yuan (81.43 million U.S. dollars) project to preserve 22 historical and cultural heritage sites in Tibet, including the Zhaxi Lhunbo Lamasery, the Jokhang, Ramogia, Sanyai and Samgya-Goutog monasteries.

Conclusion

Tibet and China have had a long and turbulent relationship. Today, the nation of Tibet does not exist. Not one foreign government officially recognizes the Tibetan government in exile. Even India recognizes that Tibet is an integral part of China. But China is suspicious of Indian and western designs. Geopolitical situations keep changing. India and the west may support a struggle for independence in Tibet. In 2006, the Dalai Lama has declared that "Tibet wants autonomy, not independence". However, the Chinese distrust him, believing that he has not really given up the quest for Tibetan independence. Talks between representatives of the Dalai Lama and the Chinese government began again in May 2008, and are still continuing. Projects such as the Qinghai—Tibet Railway have roused fears of facilitating military mobilization and Han migration. There is still ethnic imbalance in appointments and promotions to the civil and judicial services in the Tibetan Autonomous Region, with disproportionately few ethnic Tibetans appointed to these posts.

China is paranoid about the Dalai Lama and his hold on the Tibetan people. They fear that the Tibetan exiles in India may one day restart an armed freedom struggle in Tibet with Indian and Western assistance. All assurances by India and Dalai Lama that Tibet is a part of China has proved to be insufficient to allay Chinese fears. Dalai Lama and the Tibetan people in India remains a major and difficult issue in Sino-Indian relations.

China's Counter India Strategy

Beijing's "counter-India" strategy was drawn up in the 1950s. India was identified as an eventual competitor for being the pre-eminent power in Asia. The strategy is to encircle India by a ring of countries friendly to China and inject in them fears of the Indian threat. That is why China embarked on a long-term propaganda or psychological warfare employing its official media, military strategic experts and political scientists to project the "India Threat" theory among India's neighbours. China aligned with Pakistan as early as 1963 and has been a major supplier of military equipment, technology and economic aid since then. It next aligned with Bangladesh in 1976 and is today the primary supplier of military equipment and aid to Bangladesh. It next aligned with the Military Junta ruling Burma in 1988. Chinese military and economic aid has enabled the Military Junta in Myanmar to defy the US and the West and continue with its autocratic regime. China aligned with Sri Lanka in its battle with the LTTE in 2004. It has supplied military equipment and aid to Sri Lanka and encouraged Pakistan to do the same. It is providing economic aid and assisting Sri Lanka in developing its infrastructure and oil and gas resources. It is trying to align with the Maoists in Nepal. If it succeeds, Bhutan will be the only SAARC nation other than India which will not be in the Chinese camp (Refer Map 1). China is known to have denied India membership of the APEC. It also tried to keep India outside the ASEAN and the ASEAN Regional Forum (ARF). It opposes India getting a permanent seat in the UN Security Council.

Indo-US Defense Cooperation

Beijing makes no secret of its perception that it considers India to be a part of US plans to encircle China. China believes that the Indo-US defense cooperation was to counter China's regional aspirations and the US intended to form a strategic partnership with India to increase its influence in South Asia to counter China. It also considers that the US-India nuclear co-operation was part of India's ambition to become a super power and its conventional defence build-up was aimed to dominate South Asia.

Conclusion

There is no possibility of resolving the boundary issue unless both countries are ready to accept the LAC as the international border. As of today, this is highly unlikely. In fact, the indications are quite to the contrary. As per an article in *Times of India* of 10 May, 2009, Chinese patrols violated the border 270 times during 2008 which is a substantial increase over 2007. 60 border violations have taken place in the first four months of 2009, when the borders are largely snow bound during winter.

India cannot also extradite Dalai Lama and the Tibetan refugees to China.

India cannot prevent China from being friendly with its neighbours and providing them with military equipment, military aid and economic aid. No amount of sugar coating or rhetoric can hide the insurmountable nature of the problems to friendly relations between the two countries. The only option before India is to make itself militarily and economically strong enough to make China averse to a military adventure against it.

Map No. 1: China's Encirclement of India

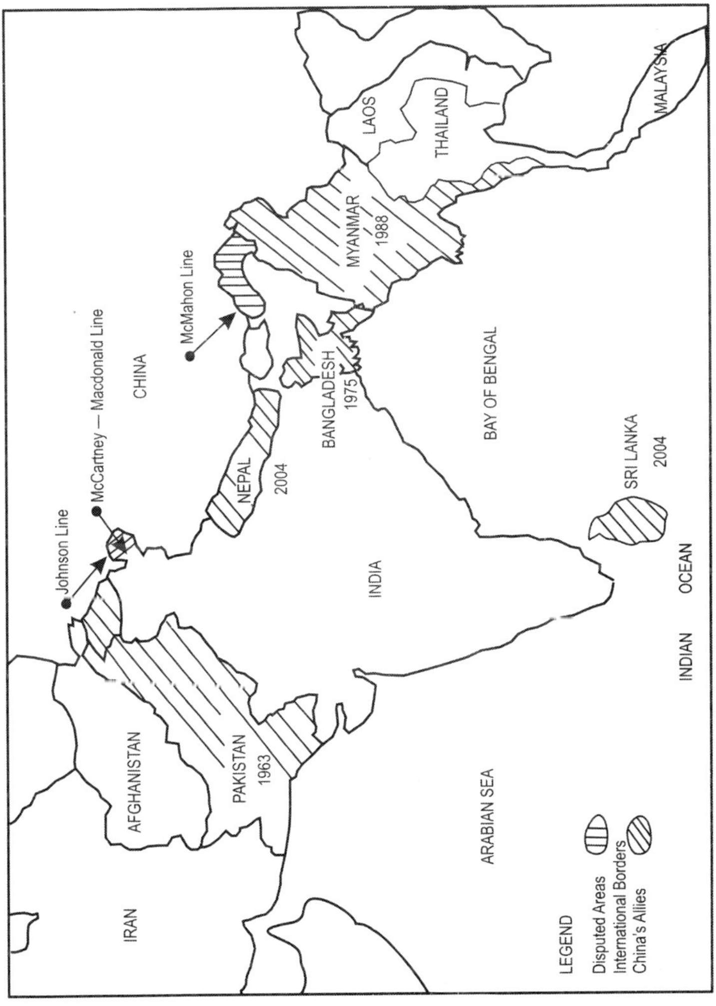

Part 2
Military Reasons for Concern

China's Military Might

3

Introduction

China's armed forces are ranked the largest in the world with a combined strength of about 2.2 million men at arms and about one million reserves. It had a military budget of US $70.2 billion in 2007, which is second only to the US. India in comparison had a budget of only about US $ 30 billion.

In its early years, the Chinese used to lay greater emphasis on quantity over quality. But in the last twenty years, it has gone all out to modernize its forces. The regular army has been reduced by about 5,00,000 men over the past few years, with the 5,00,000 being transferred to Armed Police Divisions which have been deployed on its borders. Combat effectiveness is sought to be increased by technology-intensive elements such as special forces, army aviation (transport aircraft and helicopters), surface to air missiles (SAM) and electronic warfare units. The latest operational doctrine of the PLA ground forces highlights the importance of information technology, electronic and cyber warfare and long-range precision missile strikes in future wars. The older generation command, control, and communications (C3) systems are being replaced by an integrated battlefield information networks featuring local/wide-area networks (LAN/WAN), satellite communications, unmanned aerial vehicle (drone) based surveillance and reconnaissance systems and mobile command and control centers. According to Russian experts, China's defence acquisition from Russia between 1990-96 was worth $ 26 billion. The trend has continued till the last few years but has slowed down, because China is no longer willing to accept second generation technology and the Russians are unable to decide to what extent they can part with their latest technologies. However, modernization of a large force as that of China requires time and money. So the Chinese formations are classified as Category A or Category B. Category A formations have priority for modernization.

Chinese Regular Army

China has the world's largest ground forces, currently totaling some 1.6 million personnel. The Chinese regular army consists of 18 Group Armies, which are comparable to Indian "corps" size combined arms formations. According to the International Institute of Strategic Studies' 2006 Military Balance Report, China has nine armored divisions, three mechanized infantry divisions, twenty four motorized infantry divisions, fifteen infantry divisions, two amphibious assault divisions, one mechanized infantry brigade, twenty two motorized infantry brigades, twelve armored brigades, seven artillery divisions, fourteen artillery brigades, nineteen anti-aircraft artillery (AAA) missile brigades, and ten army aviation (helicopter) regiments. The ground forces are divided among the seven military regions. The deployment of the Chinese regular Army is described below. (Please refer to Map 2). The regular army units are some times used for internal security duties like quelling the student demonstrations at the Tianaman Square and protests in Tibet and Xinjiang Provinces. They are also used in aid to civil authorities at times of natural disasters like earthquakes or floods.

Shenyang Military Region is located at the north-east corner of China and is responsible for defending its borders with Russian Federation and North Korea. This region has only one group army, the 16th and three military districts. The details of troops in this region are given below:

Group Army	Location	Divisions	Brigades/Regiments	Remarks
16th Group Army	Changhung	Armd div-1, mot inf div-1, inf div-2	Mot inf bde-1, AAA bde-1, engr regt-1	

Abbreviations used in the tables are: armd—armored, div-divisions, Mot-motorized, inf—Infantry, mech—mechanized, arty-Artillery, AAA-Anti Aircraft Artillery, engr-engineer, AD-air defence.

Beijing Military Region is responsible for the borders with Mongolia and Russia. It could be holding some of the Chinese strategic reserves. It has four groups armies, three military districts and two garrisons one of which is located in Beijing. It could be having some independent divisions. The details of troops in the region are given below:

Group Army	Location	Divisions	Brigades/ Regiments	Remarks
38th Mech Army Group	Baoding	Armd div-1, mech inf divs-3	Arty bde-1, mech AD bde-1, aviation regt-1	Category A
21st Army Group	Sensi	Armd div-1, inf div-3	Mot inf bde-1, arty bde-1, AAA bde-1, engr regt-1	
23rd Army Group	Heiliongjiang	Mot inf div-1	Mot inf bde-2, AAA bde-1, arty bde-1	
39th Mech Army Group	Liaoyang	Armd div-1, mech inf div-3	AAA bde 1, arty bde-1, helicopter regt 1	Category A

Jinan Military Region lies on China's east coast between the Beijing Military Region and the Nanjing Military Region. It is not located on any international border and could be holding Chinese strategic reserves. This region has two army groups and two military districts. Their details are given below:

Group Army	Location	Divisions	Brigades/Regiments	Remarks
20th Army Group	Qianwei	Armd div-1	Mech inf bde-1, mot inf bde-1, AAA bde-1, arty bde-1	
63rd Army Group	Taiyuang	Mot inf div-1	Armd bde-1, mot inf bde-1, inf bde-1, arty bde-1	

Map No. 2: Military Regions of China

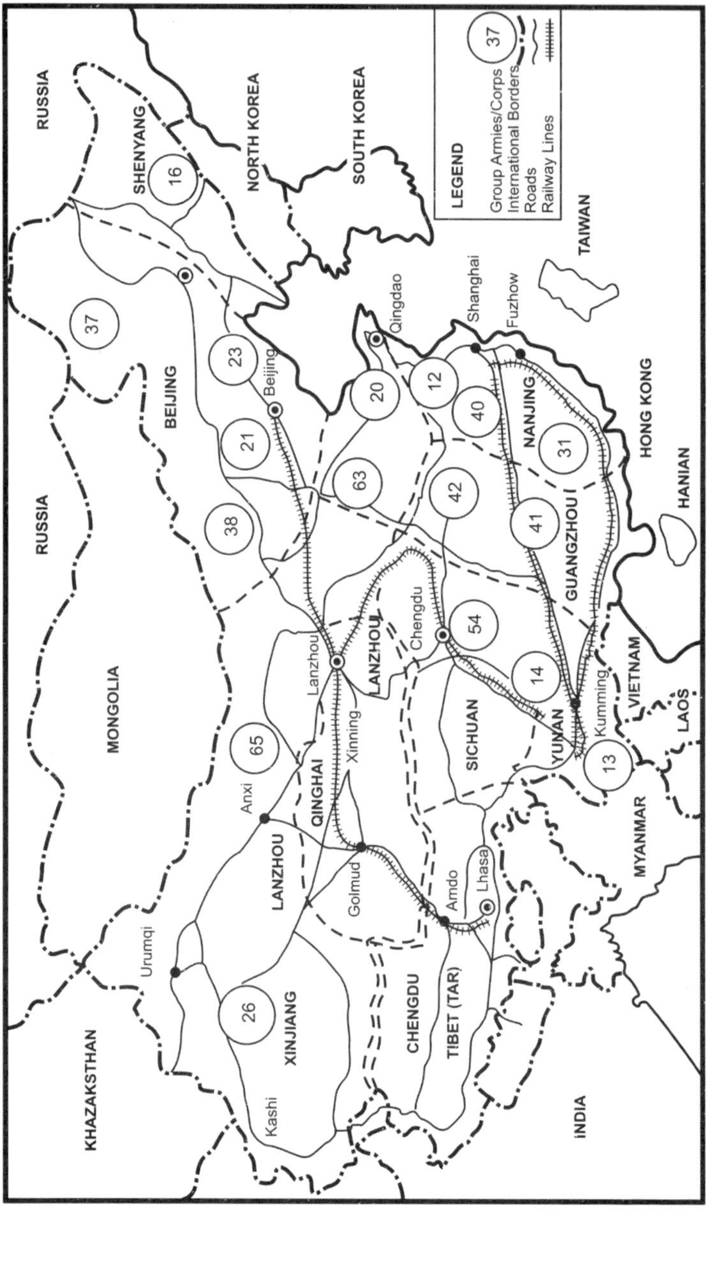

Nanjing Military Region lies on the east coast of China and is responsible for operations against Taiwan. It has four group armies and a concentration of offensive formations and amphibious capabilities. This region has four Group Armies, five military districts and the Shanghai garrison. The details of the group armies are given below:

Group Army	Location	Divisions	Brigades/ Regiments	Remarks
1st Army Group	Huzhow	Amphibious mech inf div-1, armd div-1, Arty div-1	Mot inf bde-1, AAA bde-1, engr regt-1	Category A
40th Army Group	Janzhou	Inf div-1	Armd bde-1, mot bde-2, AAA bde-1, arty bde-1, engr regt-1	Category B
31st Army Group	Xiamen	Mot inf div-1, inf div-1	Armd bde-1, AAA bde-1, arty bde-1, engr regt-1, pontoon regt-1	Category A
12th Army Group	Xuzhou	Armd div-1, inf div-1	Mot inf bde-2, AAA bde-1, arty bde-1, engr regt-1, pontoon regt-1	Category A

Guangzhou Military Region is one of the smallest military regions in terms of area. It is responsible for operations in Hong Kong, Macau and a part of China's border with Vietnam. It is also closest to Arunachal after Chengdu Military region and could provide troops for operations against India. It has two group armies, the details of which are given below. It also has four military districts and the Hong Kong and Macau garrisons.

Group Army	Location	Divisions	Brigades/ Regiments	Remarks
42nd Army Group	Hiuzhou	Amphibious mech div-1, inf div-1	Armd bde-1, AAA bde-1, engr regt-1	Category A
41st Army Group	Luizhou	Mot inf div-1, inf div-1	Armd bde-1, AAA bde-1, engr regt-1, pontoon regt-1	

Chengdu Military Region is responsible for China's borders with India, Nepal, Bhutan, Burma and a part of Vietnam and internal security of Tibetan Autonomous Region. As such this military region is of most interest to India. This Military Region is responsible for operation against India. The region has three group armies and a number of independent holding units and armed police units permanently deployed in Tibet. The details of Chinese troops deployed in Tibet are discussed in Chapter 9. The details of troops in Chengdu military region are given below. The region also has four military districts and the Chongqing garrison.

Group Army	Location	Divisions	Brigades/Regiments	Remarks
14th Group Army	Kumming	Inf div-1, arty div-1	Armd bde-1, AAA bde-1, engr regt-1, pontoon regt-1	Category B
13th Group Army	Myanmar border	Mot inf div-1, inf div-1	Armd bde-1, AAA bde-1, arty bde-1	Category A
54th Group Army	Xincheng	Light mot div-1, mot inf div-1	Armd bde-1, mech inf bde-1, arty bde-1, AAA bde-1, engr regt-1	Took part in 1962 War
Sichuan Military District		Reserve inf Div-1/Armed Police Div		Opposite eastern Arunachal
Xijang Military District		Equivalent of three Armed Police Divs	Two mot inf brigades and other support regiments	Responsible for TAR
Guizhou Military District		Reserve Inf div-1/Armed Police Div		
Yunan Military District		Reserve Inf Div-1/Armed Police Div		Borders Myanmar

Lanzhou Military Region is located in the north-west areas of China. It is responsible for defence of international borders with India (North Kashmir), Pakistan (POK), Afghanistan, Kyrgyzstan, Kazakhstan and Mongolia. It is also responsible for internal security of Xinjiang Province including Aksai Chin and Qinghai Provinces. This military regions has two Group

Armies and five Military districts. The troops deployed in this region are given below:

Army Group	location	Divisions	Brigades/ Regiments	Remarks
26th Army Group	Weifang	Armd div-1, mot inf div-1, inf div-1, arty div-1	Mot inf bde-2, AAA bde-1	
65th Army Group	Zanjakhou	Inf div-1, arty div-1	Armd bde-1, mot inf bde-2, AAA bde-1	
Shaanxi Military District				Details not available
Ghansu Military District		76 Inf Div	Inf bde 1	
Qinghai Military District		Reserve Inf div-1		
Ningxia Military District				Details not available
Xinjiang Military District		Armd div-1, mot inf div-2, Inf div 1, Reserve inf div-1		

Reserves

In times of crisis, the Chinese Army will be reinforced by activating numerous reserve units and paramilitary units. The PLA reserve component has about 1.2 to 1.5 million personnel.

Equipment

The Chinese produced Type 59 and Type 69 tanks (equivalent to Soviet T54 and T55) account for over two-thirds of the total PLA tank inventory. Second generation tanks such as the Type 88 and Type 96 have also been introduced. The latest tank is the Type 99 which entered PLA service in 2001. The PLA also operates about 2,000 light tanks including the Type 62 light tank and the Type 63 amphibious tank. The Type 63 has now been upgraded. The total tank strength is estimated to be about 7500. China also has a large number of wheeled and tracked armored personnel carriers (APCs) of both indigenous and Soviet manufacture. The fleet includes BMP1, BMP2, BMP3, Nornico Type 89, Type 93, BTR 80 and BTR 152 armored personnel carriers.

The artillery include indigenously produced 105mm and 122mm howitzers, multi-barrel rocket launchers, HN5A surface to air missiles. Infantry units are equipped with indigenously produced 60mm and 120mm mortars, and 57mm, 76mm, 106mm anti-tank weapons and the Red Arrow anti-tank missiles.

PLA's Fighting Prowess

The Korean War was the first war fought by China after independence. In 1950, the PLA attacked the US forces in the Korean Peninsula in support of North Korea. At this stage, the PLA was battle hardened due to China's long conflict with Japanese occupation, World War II and civil war with Nationalists. The PLA suffered heavy casualties but fought the technologically superior US armed forces, who had total air superiority, with skill and determination and brought them to a standstill.

The next war in which the PLA participated was the Sino-Indian conflict of 1962. In October 1962, the PLA routed the Indian Army in Ladakh and Arunachal and declared unilateral ceasefire after taking possession of over 30,000 sq km of Indian territory in about a month of fighting. The Chinese success was largely due to the total unpreparedness of the Indian Army and exceptionally poor Indian military leadership. It was also due to a total failure of the political leadership of India and government of India to assess correctly the PLA's capabilities and intentions and to build a professional well equipped armed forces that could defend its borders.

The next Chinese military adventure was against India on the Sikkim-Tibet border during 1965-67. During the period from September to December 1965, the PLA sent a number of probing missions on the entire Sikkim-Tibet border. The Indian Army responded firmly at local levels. Though details of Chinese casualties from these border clashes have not been made public, there were reports indicating that the PLA suffered "heavy" casualties against "moderate" losses by India.

Two years later, in September 1967, the PLA launched a direct attack on the Indian Army units at Nathu La, on the Sikkim-Tibet border. The six-day border skirmish from September 6 to 13, 1967 included exchange of heavy artillery fire. The PLA soldiers tried to cross the border in large numbers. The attack was repulsed at all points. The Chinese received a severe mauling in the artillery duels. Indian gunners scored several direct hits on Chinese bunkers, including a command post from where the Chinese operations were being directed. The Chinese were reported to have suffered at least twice as many casualties as the Indians in this encounter. The Nathu La episode demonstrated beyond doubt that the PLA was not invincible.

The next Chinese military adventure was the Sino-Vietnam War of 1979. China wanted "to teach a lesson" to the Vietnamese. But the PLA was badly mauled and forced to retreat. The battle hardened Vietnamese, with better strategy and motivation, were able to take on the PLA and inflict heavy casualties. The defeat made China realize that there was need to improve the fighting capabilities of the PLA. Consequently, the military modernization was accelerated.

The next Chinese military adventure was against India and is known as the Sumdorong Chu Valley incident of 1986. In mid-1986, it came to the notice of India that the PLA had built a helipad at Wandung in Sumdorong Chu Valley in Arunachal Pradesh. India reacted swiftly and the PLA had an eyeball to eyeball confrontation with the Indian Army in Sumdorong Chu Valley in August 1986. After a week of tense moments both sides mutually agreed to withdraw their forces inside their respective territories and create a no man's land.

It will thus be seen that the Chinese soldiers are not supermen. But as they say, during wars, God is usually with the side with more and larger guns.

The Chinese Air Force

The Chinese Air Force has about 250,000 personnel and 2300 fighters and ground attack aircrafts. The air force is organized into seven Military Region Air Forces and has 44 Air Divisions. It is the largest air force in Asia-Pacific region and the third largest in the world after the US and Russian Air Forces. An air division has 2 to 3 aviation regiments, each with 20 to 36 aircrafts. There are also three air borne divisions manned by the PLAAF. The Chinese Air Force is also divided into 16 Airborne Corps. Shenyang Military has four fighter divisions, two ground attack divisions and a few independent air force regiments. Beijing Military region has three fighter divisions and one air transport division. Lanzhou military region has two fighter divisions and one bomber division. Nanjing military region has three fighter divisions, one ground attack division and one bomber division. Guangzhou military region has five fighter division, one bomber division and one air transport division. The Jinan military region has two fighter divisions and one ground attack division. The Chengdu military region has only two fighter divisions. In case of a war with India, the air force in Chengdu military region will have to be beefed up with additional air divisions from Lanzhou and Guangzhou military regions.

The Air Force possesses squadrons of F6, F9 and Jian 7 (J7) fighter jets and JY 11-3D air surveillance radars. The JF-10 and J-17 (Thunder) aircraft are the state of art fighters produced in China. Apart from the above there have been acquisitions from Russia including SU-27 aircraft along with production agreement. The best combat aircrafts in China's PLAAF are Russian SU-30 MK III and indigenously built, 4th generation JF 10 and J-17 fighters.

Chinese Navy

China marked the 60th anniversary of the founding of its navy with a spectacular parade in the seas off the northern port city of Qingdao in May 2009. The PLA Navy has about 290,000 personnel. It has a fleet of about 172 combat ships including 26 destroyers, 49 frigates, 14 corvettes, 60 submarines and a large number of fast patrol boats. The government has pushed a vigorous modernization program for the navy. The emphasis is on developing vessels at home or buying them from Russia. It has also built or is planning to build its own submarines, including nuclear-powered ones based on upgraded designs, to replenish its aged fleet. Many of the newer submarines will be based at Hanian, an island province near the recent confrontation between a U.S. navy ship and Chinese warships. (See Map 2). Some of its latest equipment are the Ying Ji missile and C-102 ship-to-ship missiles and the indigenous F 22 P state of art frigate.

Taiwan remains the focus of Chinese military concerns and its naval strategy. China believes that as its international political and economic stature grows, it must have a navy capable of protecting its expanding global interests. Much of navy's growing budget has gone to building or buying new warships, submarines and other technology required for building a "blue sea navy". Beijing recently demonstrated that ambition by sending warships to help an international effort against pirates menacing commercial ships off the Somali coast. It is seeking to establish its presence in the Indian Ocean by modernizing naval bases at Kyaukpyu, the Coco islands and Sittwe (Akyab) in Myanmar, Chittagong and Kutubdia Island in Bangladesh and Gwadar in Pakistan. It is also improving the Hambantota port in Sri Lanka which could be used as a supply base for the Chinese Navy (Refer Map 5).

The Chinese Navy is organized into three major fleets, the North Sea Fleet with its headquarters at Qingdao, the East Sea Fleet headquartered at Ningbo, and the South Sea Fleet headquartered in Zhanjiang. The navy includes a Coastal Defence Force of 35,000, 56,000 Naval Infantry/Marines including two multi-arm marine brigades and a 56,000 strong naval air arm operating several hundred land-based aircraft and ship based helicopters.

Indigenous production of its nuclear powered submarine, the Type-093 has commenced. The Type-094 nuclear powered and nuclear JL-2 missile armed submarine, the new Shan Class submarines, the DF-31 and DF-31A intercontinental ballistic missiles (ICBMS) are being developed. An agreement has been concluded with Russians for 3 Sovremenny class destroyers and 12 Kilo class submarines.

Strategic Missile Forces

China started its nuclear program in 1955. The first nuclear test was conducted on 16 October 1964. The Second

Artillery Corps was formed on 1 July 1966. The Second Artillery Corps (SAC) is the strategic missile forces of the PLA. It controls China's nuclear and conventional strategic missiles. China's total nuclear arsenal size is estimated to be between 100 and 400 nuclear weapons. The SAC has approximately 90,000 to 120,000 personnel and six ballistic missile divisions. The six divisions are independently deployed in different military regions and have a total of 15 to 20 missile brigades. It is estimated that China has about 100-160 liquid fueled ICBMs capable of striking the United States. It has approximately 100 to 150 IRBMs capable of striking Russia or Eastern Europe. China also possesses several hundred tactical SRBM with ranges between 300 and 600 km. China is reported to have deployed around one thousand M-9 missiles on its eastern coast, targeting Taiwan. As a part of its "counter-India" strategy, China has deployed medium range nuclear ballistic missiles like the DF-21 and DF-21A to cover most of India. Its growing fleet of it's nuclear submarines is eventually going to patrol the Indian Ocean. The CIA has said in 2002 that China will quadruple or quintuple its number of long-range nuclear missiles by 2015.

Space Based System

The PLA has deployed a number of space based systems for military purposes. These include the intelligence satellite systems like the Zi Yan series and the militarily designated Jian Bing series, synthetic aperture satellites (SAR) such as Jian Bing-5, Bei Dou satellite navigation system and secured communication satellites. The PLA has started the development of an anti-ballistic and anti-satellite system in the 1960s, code named Project 640, including ground based lasers, and anti-satellite missiles. On January 11, 2007 China conducted a successful test of an anti-satellite missile, with an SC-19 class KKV.

Cyber Warfare Capability

Chinese cyber warfare is meant to disable the opponent's communication systems. China has rapidly developed it's cyber warfare capability. In the last two years, China's military hackers defaced India's Defence Ministry and Bhaba Atomic Research Centre (BARC) websites. Although no real damage was done, these are precursors. Chinese hackers have also occasionally hacked into Pentagon and White House computer systems. Recently, a cyber attack, possibly by North Koreans, disabled many computer networks in the US and South Korea for almost one week.

Defence Production Capability

Right from independence in October 1949, the Chinese strongly believed in self-reliance in military equipment. Initially, a considerable amount of Soviet technology was transferred to China. The Soviet technology transfers stopped coming from the mid-1950s onwards. But since 1971, Chinese have been shopping in the international market for weapon systems and spent considerable amount of its money in modernizing its armed forces. Since 1980, China is a major producer and exporter of weapon systems. Some may question the performance of weapon systems that China is selling in the international market. But Pakistan, North Korea, Bangladesh, Sri Lanka and Iran have bought their equipment and are equipping their armies with the same. Chinese equipment saw action in the Iraq-Iran war of the 1990s. The Iranians used the Silkworm missiles from China quite successfully to confront Iraq.

Defence industries in China produce sufficient surplus for China to have become a leading arms supplier in the world. Economic reforms introduced by leader Deng Xiaoping in 1979 resulted in major changes in China's arms industry during the 1980s. The reforms enabled individual government agencies and public institutions, including those within the military, to set up their own commercial companies. As a consequence, numerous sub-units within the military complex began operating profit-making companies involved in arms manufacturing, imports and exports. The largest Chinese arms companies include:

- Norinco, China North Industries Corporation.

- China Poly Group Corporation, which is one of the largest Chinese arms exporting companies and is operated by PLA's General Staff Department.
- Xinxing Corporation, which is operated by the PLA General Logistics Department.

Chinese defence industries have been assisted by western firms who have provided technological assistance for money. One example is the Z-10 attack helicopter developed by China Helicopter Research and Development Institute. China is buying skills and off the shelf technology and routing them into military programs.

Chinese arms deals often involve an exchange of weapons for raw materials. In the 1990s, the PLA exported arms to Iran in return for oil. China is the major arms supplier to its allies like Pakistan, Myanmar, Bangladesh and Sri Lanka. China is also a major supplier of arms to Sudan, Liberia, Zimbabwe, Venezuela etc. The exports include small arms and light weapons, artillery guns, tanks, armored personnel carriers, anti-tank missiles, fighter aircraft and helicopters. The exports are worth billions of US dollars and help China get political support in these countries.

Conclusion

It will be seen from above that the Chinese Armed forces are the largest in the world and its air force and navy are the third largest after the US and Russians. With over 2 trillion US dollars as its foreign exchange reserves, it is determined to make use of its economic resources to become the number one military power in the world. It may take fifteen to twenty years to achieve this goal. But that is not much of a solace to India which is falling behind every year.

An assessment of Chinese military ambitions against India and what China can deploy against India is discussed in Chapter 10.

China's Relations with Pakistan

4

Background

Pakistan became the third non-communist country and the first Muslim country to recognize Peoples Republic of China in 1950. Diplomatic relation between the two countries was established in 1951. Pakistan became an Islamic Republic in 1956. Just two years later, the military took control of the nation. Field Marshal Ayub Khan became President. Ayub took advantage of the cold war and established close relations with the US and the West. Pakistan joined two formal military alliances, the Baghdad Pact (later known as CENTO) which included Iran, Iraq and Turkey to defend the Middle-East and the Persian Gulf against the Soviet Union and SEATO which covered south-east Asia. As a result, America provided substantial military aid in the form of small arms, tanks, anti-tank weapons, artillery and fighter aircraft.

Pakistan did not assist China in the Sino-Indian conflict of 1962. Defence cooperation between Pakistan and China began in 1963 when Pakistan ceded a part of Pakistan Occupied Kashmir (POK) in the Karakorum mountains as a part of their border settlement pact of March 3, 1963. Since then, China has emerged as Pakistan's single most trusted and enduring military ally. This cooperation is based on their mutual antagonism towards India. It is also beneficial to both the countries. Pakistan is a major market for Chinese weapons. Pakistan does not have a strong domestic industrial, scientific and technological base. China supplies Pakistan with cheap products and technologies. It also provides the required political and moral support to Pakistan at the UN when required. In return China is given access to western technologies that arrive in Pakistan. Both are ruled by authoritarian regimes and both have military dominated politics which makes mutual dealings easier. The United States stopped military aid to both India and Pakistan during the Indo-Pak War of 1965. This was responsible for an increasing emphasis within Pakistan for self-reliance in defence production. This also pushed Pakistan closer towards China in an attempt to diversify its sources of weapons and other equipment. Pakistan defied considerable American pressure to seek a strategic relationship with China. China provided diplomatic support to Pakistan in its war with India in 1965 and 1971. The Karakorum Highway linking northern Pakistan to Western China through Pakistan Occupied Kashmir and the Khunjareb Pass was completed in 1978. Cordial relations with China have been a pillar of Pakistan's foreign policy. China strongly supported Pakistan's opposition to Soviet involvement in Afghanistan in 1970. Pakistan perceives China as a regional counterweight to India and USSR.

The Long History of Defence Cooperation

The first formal step towards Sino-Pak defence cooperation was taken soon after 1965 war between India and Pakistan. China provided technical and financial assistance for setting up an ordnance factory at Dhaka, East Pakistan. This ordnance factory was commissioned in November 1970. The Heavy Mechanical Complex (HMC), the biggest undertaking of its type in Pakistan, was set up at Taxila in 1979 with the help of Chinese assistance and expertise. The Heavy Forge Factory (HFF) at this complex has proved crucial for Pakistan's defence production needs. Pakistan and China signed the Sino-Pak Memorandum of Understanding (MoU) for a ten year cooperation in procurement, R & D, technology transfer and co-production in June 1990. This understanding has got a fresh lease of life ever since the US imposed sanctions for carrying out nuclear tests. Some major projects which have been undertaken under this agreement are discussed in the succeeding paragraphs.

Production of Armored Vehicles

China provided assistance to Pakistan in setting up facilities at the Heavy Rebuild Factory (HRF) at Taxila which not only provides for the overhauling of Chinese Type-59 main battle tanks (MBTs) but also upgrading critical components of these tanks' such as its fire control systems, thermal sight and electronic systems. In the 1980s, HRF started license production of the Chinese Type-69 MBTs. Later, a protocol was signed between China and Pakistan to set up facilities for the license production of Chinese Type-69 II BMPs. China's weapon production company Norinco has also helped Pakistan in the manufacture of Chinese T-69 and T-85 II MBT and M-113 Armored Personnel Carriers. Al-Khalid Main Battle Tank (Pakistan's own MBT) project began in 1988 at Taxila with Chinese collaboration and was completed in 1992. The 'Al-Khalid' is also called MBT-2000. Primary prototypes produced in China were fielded for trials in August 1991. Production is in progress since 2001. Some of these tanks have been provided to Bangladesh and Sri Lanka.

Production of Aircraft

The Pakistan Aeronautical Complex at Kamra was also established with Chinese assistance. The F-6 Rebuild Factory was set up as a turnkey project by China and became operational in November 1980. The Chinese F-6 fighter aircraft became the mainstay of the Pakistan Air Force (PAF) after the American F-86 Sabers were phased out. China later built overhauling facilities for the F-6 fighter and the Tumansky RD-9B-8II turbojet engines in Pakistan. Later, China also expanded this factory to undertake the overhauling of FT-5, FT-6 and FT-7s Chinese fighter aircraft. When the F-6s were phased out, the facility was diversified towards maintenance and overhaul of the F-7Ps. The Light Aircraft Manufacturing Factory (LAMF), another turnkey project was completed by China in June 1981. It was meant for producing complete airframes and eventual production of light aircraft.

By September 1983, this facility started licensed production of SAAB Scania MF-1-17 (locally known as Mushshak). The Karakoram-8 (or K-8) jet trainer aircraft was a joint venture between the China National Aero-Technology Import and Export Corporation (CATIC), China Nanchang Aircraft Manufacturing Company (CNAMC) and the Pakistan Aeronautical Complex (PAC). It was established in 1986. The maiden flight of the K-8 jet trainers took place in November 1990. As an interim measure, the two countries signed an agreement for Pakistan's purchase of six K-8 jet trainers from China. These were delivered beginning from July 1994. But by the time prototypes became ready in 1994, Pakistan had decided against building its own assembly line and went on to buy them from China. The JF-17 Thunder aircraft developed with Chinese assistance is being produced in Pakistan since 2008.

Development of Missiles

Pakistan's missile development program was started in 1986 when Pakistan started assembling the Chinese RBS-70 Mk 1 and Mk 2 air defence missiles systems. Collaboration in the area of longer range missiles with the Chinese began once Pakistan became involved in financing their M-9 and M-11 missiles programs. General Mirza Aslam Beg is on record for having told the press after a visit to Beijing in 1987 that China's Red Arrow anti-tank missiles were better than US TOW-11. Chinese help is suspected to be responsible for Pakistan's successful testing in early 1989 of its Hatf II missile with a 300 km range. The US intelligence agencies have reported that China has transferred about 30 or more of its intermediate range M-11 missiles to Pakistan. Both China and Pakistan have repeatedly denied this report. China has also provided significant assistance to Pakistan's ballistic missile program in the year 2000 which has put the country on the road to serial production of Short Range Ballistic Missiles like Shaheen-1 and Haider-1. China continues to provide significant assistance to Pakistan's ballistic missile program and Pakistan is moving toward serial production of solid propellant Short Range Ballistic Missiles.

Arms Supplies to Pakistan

China has been the most important supplier of arms to Pakistan since the mid 1960s. China accounted for over one-third of Pakistan's arms imports during 1966-80. The US sanctions made Pakistan more dependent on arms imports from China. As a result, China has supplied Pakistan with more than 1,600 main battle tanks, 400 combat aircraft and about 40 naval vessels. China, in fact, has developed such a stake in supplying arms to Pakistan that it has often flouted its commitment to both the Nuclear Non-Proliferation Treaty (NPT) as also the Missile Technology Control Regime (MTCR). Given these realities there is no reason to presume that the China-Pakistan military nexus will not increase over time.

Some of the important weapon systems supplied over the years to Pakistan army include about 1000 T-59 MBTs, 600 T-82 MBTs, 100 T-63 light tanks, 100 122mm self-propelled artillery guns. The Pakistani air force has been supplied with over 140 F-6 fighters, 140 Q-5 fighters, 100 F-7 fighter bombers and an unspecified number of IL28 bombers. The F-7 are multi-role combat aircraft with a range of 850 km and can reach most cities in north-west India. The delivery of 250 JF17 fighters and 30 J-10 fighters (based on American F 16 design) was discussed during General Tariq Majid's visit to China in January 2009. The Pakistani navy has been supplied with 12 Shanghai Class patrol boats, 4 Hainan Class patrol boats, 4 Huchan class and 4 Hegu Class fast attack craft and 2 Romeo class destroyers. China also promised to expedite the delivery of four F-22 frigates. Two of the same were delivered in 2008. The Chinese are also helping Pakistan in developing one of its key naval bases at Gwadar.

China-Pakistan Nuclear Cooperation

We have to thank China for making Pakistan a nuclear weapons power. China-Pakistan nuclear cooperation began in the early 1980s. It is believed that China assisted Pakistan in developing nuclear weapons prior to its joining the NPT in 1992. In 1983, US intelligence agencies reported that China had transferred a complete nuclear weapon design to Pakistan, along with enough weapon grade uranium for two nuclear weapons. China also helped Pakistan operate its Kahuta uranium enrichment plant. In 1986, China concluded a comprehensive nuclear cooperation agreement with Pakistan. China also involved Pakistani scientists in a nuclear test at its Lop Nor test site in 1989. It is believed that China carried out a nuclear test for Pakistan at the same site in 1990. It was because of Chinese assistance that Pakistan could carry out successful nuclear weapons tests within a day of India's nuclear tests on 26 May, 1998.

China and Pakistan have cooperated in setting up nuclear power plants in Pakistan. On December 31, 1991, China signed a contract to build the Chashma 300 MW nuclear power reactor for Pakistan. As China pledged to only transfer materials to safeguarded facilities, Pakistan signed an IAEA safeguards (limited-scope) agreement for the reactor at Chashma. In 1993, China and the International Atomic Energy Agency (IAEA) signed an agreement to apply IAEA safeguards for a Chinese nuclear power plant sold to Pakistan. Pakistan's Chashma Nuclear Power Plant, which is built by Chinese firms, was commissioned in November 1999. China continues providing equipment and technology for the construction of a 40 MW reactor at Khushab. US officials fear that the reactor could provide Pakistan with plutonium for its weapons program. In March 2003, China and Pakistan signed an MOU to construct phase 2 of the Chashma facility, a second 300 MW nuclear power plant. The exact progress of the project is not known.

Economic Cooperation

China and Pakistan signed a free trade agreement in 2008. It is the first such agreement signed by the two countries. As a direct result, China will open new industries in Pakistan and Pakistan would be offered free trade zones in China. Pakistan and China have agreed to build first ever train routes along the Karakorum Highway. China may be interested in the oil and gas reserves in Baluchistan province of Pakistan. China is ready to make a large investment in Pakistan's chronically weak manufacturing sector. It is also the only worthwhile partner of

Pakistan in defence technology and production. Pakistan's economy is registering a nosedive on major economic indicators. The Pakistani Rupee currently stands at 80 against one US dollar whereas just six months ago, one dollar was equal to Rs. 60. The country's trade deficit stands at 12 billion dollars, which is the highest ever in its 61 year old history. With the global financial crisis pushing it to the brink and its strategic relations with the US strained, Pakistan is once again returning to an old trump card, i.e. China. Pakistan is using the China card to put pressure on the US and get more concessions. President Asif Ali Zardari visited Beijing to get crucial Chinese investments in the country. China has promised to help cash strapped Pakistan avert a financial disaster.

Diplomatic Cooperation

The US-Pakistan relations improved after terror strikes on the US on September 11, 2001. President Bush considered Pakistan's help in fighting the Taliban as indispensable. President Obama feels the same way and has increased US economic aid three-folds. But Pakistan continues to look up to China for most of its military and nuclear development requirements. The strategic alliance between China and Pakistan is designed to denying India the predominant power status in the South Asia. Mr. G. Parthasarathy, former Indian High Commissioner to Pakistan has claimed in an article in *Times of India* that China supports Pakistan unconditionally. Though it did not veto the UN resolution to ban the Pakistani terrorist organization, Jaish-e-Mohammad, after the terrorist strike on Mumbai on 26/11, it continues anti-India campaign in its domestic media. China's Vice President assured Pakistan that it would continue to support Pakistan at the UN. In fact, China supported Pakistan's stand at the UN that the evidence submitted by India, against Jaish-e-Mohammad chief Hafeez Saeed regarding his involvement in terrorist strike in Mumbai on 26/11/2009, was not adequate to prosecute him in a court of law. In 2005, China was instrumental in Pakistan getting the status of an observer at the Shanghai Cooperation Organization. India enjoys the same status. More recently, Pakistan played a key role in China attaining a similar status with the South Asian Association for Regional Cooperation (SAARC).

Conclusion

China has long been one of Pakistan's closest regional partners, with Beijing looking to Islamabad as a counterbalance to India. A sizable section of Pakistanis have little faith in the reliability of relations with Washington beyond the exigency of the present conflict in Afghanistan. China is the only country in the world that has helped Pakistan set up a nuclear power reactor and is open to Pakistani requests for more reactors. China has also made a visible contribution to Pakistan's progress in several civil and defence related sectors.

China seeks Pakistan's help in neutralizing Islamic terrorists in its Xingjiang Province where more than 1000 incidents of arson and riots were reported last year. Even though Pakistan was not able to help China by eliminating the terrorist camps in the then Taliban controlled Afghanistan, it helped in locating scores of Uighur separatists from Xinjiang Province in a training camp in the Gilgit area of POK. The separatists were handed over to the Chinese who promptly executed them. Diplomatic cooperation is also beneficial to China. Chinese presence at Gwadar would help Chinese to keep track of US naval ships in the Gulf. Pakistan is also the geopolitical hub for bringing China, the Gulf including Iran and Africa into a thriving economic interaction.

Despite the Chinese desire for stronger ties with Pakistan, there are two main hurdles. The first major hurdle in this regard is lack of security in Pakistan. China has provided some $450 million to fund the new port of Gawadar in Baluchistan province not far from the ultra strategic straits of Hormuz, hoping it would provide Chinese ships direct access to the Gulf and Central Asian states. However, a number of Chinese engineers working in the port have been abducted and killed by unknown attackers in recent years, forcing the Chinese companies working in the project to leave. The second is the Talibanaization of Pakistan which is a direct threat to the security of Xinjiang Province which has a substantial Muslim population.

Some analysts argue that no matter what assistance Beijing can offer, America remains indispensable for Pakistan. Improving relations with China doesn't mean that Pakistan is severing its ties with the US. Relations between the US and Pakistan seems to be improving. The Pakistan government and army is acting against the Taliban and the US has trebled its non-military aid to Pakistan to $1.5 billion per year. As long as Pakistan can balance its relationship with China and the US and play one against the other, it will reap great benefits.

In spite of its close relations with Pakistan, China has not militarily intervened in the Indo-Pak wars of 1965 and 1971. It is possible that China did not consider itself strong enough to intervene in 1965. Further, in 1965, Pakistan was much closer to US than China. In 1971, India waited till December to start operations to liberate Bangladesh. By then, most of the mountain passes along the LAC had closed. Myanmar was hostile to China and northern Myanmar could not be used for operations. Hence, China could not have intervened militarily even if it had wanted to. However, things have changed. China today is a far greater military and economic power than what it was in 1971. Military infrastructure in Yunnan Province of China is well developed. Myanmar is now firmly in Chinese camp. So, there is no guarantee that it will not support Pakistan in the future. Pakistan has a pathological hatred for India and always demands that the US and the West treat it and India as equals. It is possible that China will take advantage of this hatred and try to cut India to size at an appropriate time. The possible scenario in such an eventuality is discussed in Chapter 10.

China's Relations with Bangladesh

5

Background

To start with, China's relations with Bangladesh were dictated by its friendly relations with Pakistan. It was against secession of East Pakistan and the struggle for independence launched by the people of Bangladesh. China supported Pakistan against the Mukti Bahini during the Bangladesh Liberation War of 1971. However, the support to Pakistan was restricted to political and moral support. China could not intervene militarily into the conflict as the operations started in December when the passes on the LAC were snowbound. In 1972, China exercised its veto power as a permanent member of the UN Security Council to block Bangladesh's entry into the UN. Bangladesh under Sheikh Mujibur Rehman had aligned itself with India and the Soviet Union, both of whom had strained relations with Pakistan and China. Following the assassination of Mujibur Rehman and overthrow of the Awami League government, the equation changed. Pakistan warmed towards Bangladesh after the overthrow of Mujibur Rehman and diplomatic relations were established between the two countries in 1975-76. Pakistan's allies such as Saudi Arabia and China followed suit. A preliminary agreement between China and Bangladesh to establish diplomatic and economic relations was signed in late 1975 and duly ratified in 1976. The then President of Bangladesh, Ziaur Rahman, made an official visit to China in 1977. By the mid-1980s, China had forged close commercial and cultural ties with Bangladesh and also supplied it with military aid and equipment. In 2002, the Chinese Premier Wen Jiabao made an official visit to Bangladesh and both countries declared 2005 as the "Bangladesh-China Friendship Year".

1975-2008

China did not accord diplomatic recognition to Bangladesh till 1975 when Pakistan did the same. Initially, China's relations with Bangladesh were being determined by Pakistan's foreign policy considerations. However, political and strategic realities soon took over and China made serious attempts to wean over Bangladesh from India's influence. Bangladesh became a part of the Chinese game plan to encircle India. Bangladesh thus became a major recipient of Chinese arms. China has assured Bangladesh of enhanced military and economic assistance. Bangladesh on its part endorsed the one China policy of Beijing and considered the recent incidents in Tibet as an internal matter of China.

In 2006, Dhaka emerged as one of the prime buyers of weapons made in China. China sold 65 large caliber artillery systems, 16 combat aircraft and 114 missiles and related equipment to Bangladesh in 2005 besides small arms and 82 mm mortars. In 2008, Bangladesh set up a missile launch pad near the Chittagong Port with assistance from China. Bangladesh performed its maiden missile test on May 12, 2008 with active participation of Chinese experts. It successfully test-fired a ship based anti-ship cruise missile C-802 A with a strike range of 120 km from a frigate near Kutubdia Island in the Bay of Bengal. The frigate was a 1500 ton Chinese built Jianghu class warship commissioned into the Bangladesh Navy and the C-802A missile, according to experts, is a modified version of Chinese Ying Ji missile.

Bangladesh is all set to build its own missile arsenal. The caretaker government in Dhaka is in the process of clinching a deal with an integrated European company MBDA for buying OTOMAT MK-II surface-to-air missiles and launch systems. These missiles can carry a payload of 210 kg and can hit targets 180 km away. In addition, highly-placed intelligence sources say, the Bangladesh Air Force is negotiating with

Turkish arms dealer ASELSAN to buy the Shorad (Short Range Air Defence) system and 3D air defence radars during 2009.

Bangladesh-China Defence Co-operation

A Defence Cooperation Agreement was signed between Bangladesh and China during the visit of Bangladesh Prime Minister, Begum Khaleda Zia to China in 2002. The new agreement was to help institutionalize the existing accords in defence sector and to consolidate the existing piecemeal agreements to enhance cooperation in training, maintenance and some areas in production that had existed since the early eighties. The purpose of Defence Cooperation Agreement was to meet present day upgradation and modernization needs of Bangladesh's defence forces. It was claimed that this defence umbrella agreement was not directed against any country and would not affect Bangladesh's relations with India. The major significance of the Defence Cooperation Agreement is that it is the first such agreement ever signed by Bangladesh in its history.

Defence Cooperation Agreements are normally signed when countries perceive enhanced threat from a country, in this case, clearly India. It is possible that Bangladesh fears retaliation in response to its territories being used for proxy war and terrorism against India. Bangladesh is conscious of the fact that its territory is being used by Pakistan's ISI, Al Qaeda and other fundamentalist Muslim groups for anti-India activities. India has cautioned Bangladesh on this count. The significance of Indian military escalation in 2002 and in 2008 against Pakistan would not have been lost on Bangladesh. Bangladesh therefore seems to have taken out an insurance policy from China to cater for increased threat perceptions in the India specific context.

The agreement also helps Pakistan's strategic designs against India, because Bangladesh's enhanced military profile with Chinese aid would divert some of India's strategic military assets from the West to the East and lower the pressure on Pakistan. Rising Islamic fundamentalism in Bangladesh makes it easier to use Bangladesh territory for intensifying Pakistan's proxy war on India's Eastern peripheries. This trend has somewhat reduced with the pro India Awami League coming to power. But this could be a temporary phase.

China's strategic interests are also served by the Bangladesh-China Defence Cooperation Agreement. The agreement could more aptly be termed as "Bangladesh-China Treaty of Friendship and Strategic Cooperation" with similar intent as the Indo-Soviet Treaty of Friendship and Cooperation of 1971. As a result of the Agreement, China gets a strategic toe hold on India's Eastern flank in Bangladesh. China's strategic encirclement of India is enhanced through the treaty. China could start developing the Chittagong Naval Base on the lines of Gwader in Pakistan and in return get naval bases in Bangladesh.

Strategic Implications of the Agreement for India

Has India taken cognizance of the Agreement and revised its threat perception in the East? I earnestly hope we have. Before discussing the strategic implications, I would like to draw the reader's attention to the phenomenal if not alarming growth of the armed forces of Bangladesh which I had noticed while in service before my retirement in 1991. India cannot ignore the strategic embrace of Bangladesh by China. Bangladesh's enhanced military capabilities will have to be factored in India's future military plans. India will also have to cater for the worst case scenario of China-Pakistan-Bangladesh military collusion in the context of any Indo-Pak or Sino-Indian conflict. India's lines of communications in the North East region after Siliguri will become extremely vulnerable, particularly due to threat of disruption due to sabotage by insurgent elements based in Bangladesh.

Military Build-up in Bangladesh

Bangladesh Army started with a nucleus of Bengali deserters from the Pakistan Army, paramilitary personnel, police and civilians who had fought with the Mukti Bahini in the War of Liberation of 1970-71. Bangladesh Army has expanded considerably since its formation on December 26, 1971. Between 1973 and 1975, the army absorbed most of the 28,000 personnel who had been detained in Pakistani jails for the duration of the war of independence. When General Ershad assumed power in 1982, army strength had stabilized at about 70,000 troops. Starting in 1985, Ershad accelerated the transition from martial law to elected civilian government. The army then experienced another spurt in growth. As per the official website of the Bangladesh Army, it has about 1,00,000 troops.

Till 1974-75, Bangladesh did not have a single infantry division. Today, the Bangladesh Army has six strategically located divisions. The 9 Infantry Division is located at Savar on the outskirts of Dhaka. It has an armored regiment. It has played a central role in staging coups and maintaining military governments once they were in power. The 24 Infantry Division is located at Chittagong. It has four infantry brigades and has conducted counter insurgency operations against tribal guerrillas in the Chittagong Hills since the late 1970s. The 55 Infantry division has it headquarters at Jessore. The 11 Infantry Division is located at Bogra, the 33 Infantry Division is at Comilla. Each of these divisions has an armor regiment. In April 1988, a sixth infantry division, the 66 Infantry Division was formally established with headquarters at Rangpur and plans were in place to raise its armor regiment. The formations include sixteen infantry brigades, one armoured brigade of two regiments and two armor regiments, three artillery brigade of two artillery regiments each and possibly three other artillery regiments, one engineer brigade and six engineering battalions, and various support elements, such as signals, medical services, and ordnance. As per the official website of Bangladesh Army, a seventh infantry division Headquarters has also been raised. However, it does not indicate where this division is located. The major army cantonments are at Saidpur, Rajshahi, Jamalpur, Sylhet, Thakurganj, Kushtia etc. The location of these units is shown on Map 3. The Ministry of Defence and Army Headquarters should be well aware of the latest strengths and deployment of the Bangladesh Army.

The Bangladesh Military Academy is located at Bhatiary, near Chittagong. The Defence Services Command and Staff College founded in Dhaka in 1977. Bangladeshi military officers were undergoing specialized training in Pakistan and China. Some also do various courses in India and provide information on our equipment and operational doctrines to Pakistani and Chinese intelligence.

Map No. 3: Map of Bangladesh

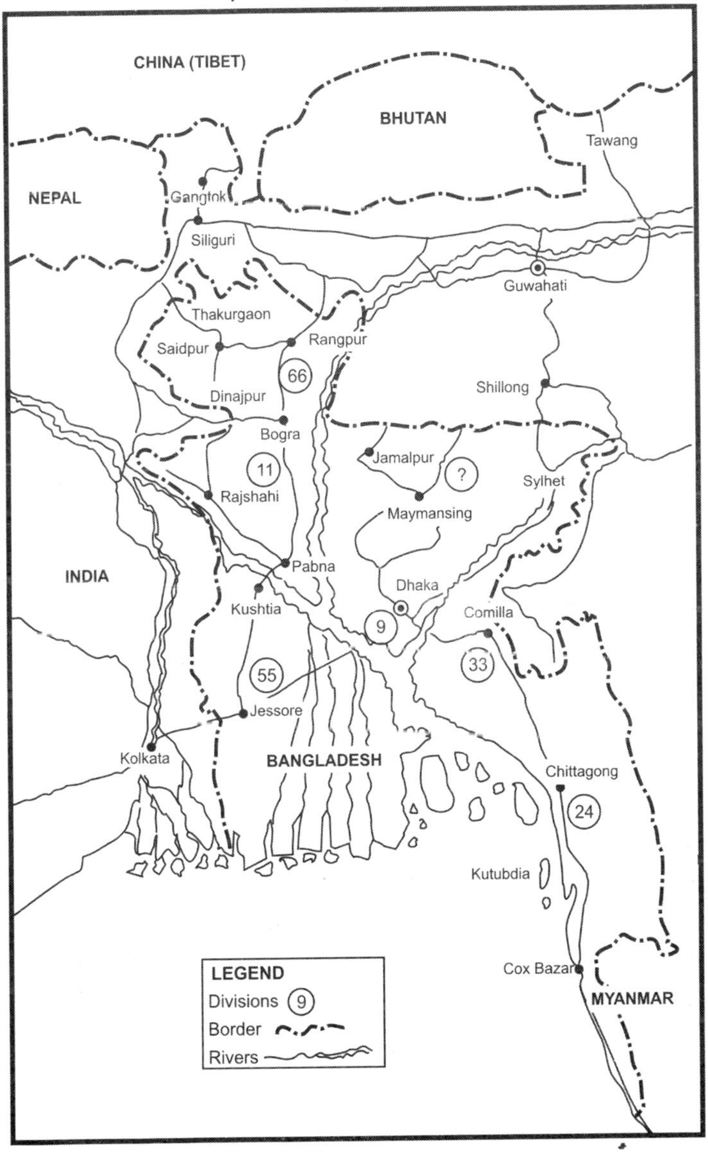

To start with, the Bangladesh Army was very poorly equipped. But that has all changed with the Chinese military aid. Bangladesh's Armed Forces today are predominantly equipped with Chinese military hardware. The Bangladesh Army's tanks and light tanks are of Chinese origin. The Bangladesh Navy's frigates and patrol crafts are mostly Chinese. The Bangladesh Air Force's combat aircraft are all Chinese. In short China has forged Bangladesh into a military-equipment client state like Pakistan. The army has about 180 Chinese tanks of Type 59, Type 69, T54 and T55. It also has 40 Type 62 light tanks and some armored personnel carriers. The artillery is equipped with 105mm and 122mm howitzers, multi-barrel rocket launchers, HN5A surface to air missiles. Infantry units are equipped with 60mm and 120mm mortars, and 57mm, 76mm, 106mm anti-tank weapons and the Red Arrow anti-tank missiles.

The Bangladesh Air Force has a current strength of about 10,000 personnel. It has twelve operational squadrons operating from three air bases located near Dhaka, Chittagong and Jessore. These include three fighter squadrons equipped with Chinese F-7, one squadron of Mig 29s, one fighter bomber or ground attack squadron equipped with Chinese A-5s, one transport squadron, three helicopter squadrons and three training squadrons.

Bangladesh Navy had a strength of about 11,000 personnel in 2000. It has four frigates (one Chinese and three older ones), ten fast attack crafts (missile) of Chinese Huangfen and Hegu class, eight fast attack craft (Torpedo) of Chinese Huchuan and P-4 class, five mine sweepers and a number of other ships. The Bangladesh navy is also reported to have acquired two Chinese F-22 class frigates.

Analysis of Military Build-up in Bangladesh

President Ershad had clearly stated that India was the only adversary of Bangladesh and its only threat. The Khaleda Zia Regime which followed appears to have the same perception. She initiated the "Bangladesh-China Treaty of Friendship and Strategic Cooperation" and military build-up in Bangladesh continued under her regime.

Let us look at the defence requirements of Bangladesh. Pakistan had three infantry divisions for the defence of East Pakistan and inducted a force during the 1971 War. This force should have been adequate to hold the six odd divisions that India could muster for the 1971 war of liberation. In reality, Pakistani Army in East Pakistan was defeated not because of lack of troops but, because of poor military leadership and strategy, surrendering air superiority to the Indians within three days and a hostile population which assisted the liberating forces. So, why does Bangladesh require such a huge army which a poor country like Bangladesh can ill afford? Why has it raised seven infantry divisions, almost double of what Pakistan had in 1971? This is all the more surprising as Indian divisions in the east have been reduced by one division since 1971. It would appear that Bangladesh is working towards acquiring a strategic reserve capability of up to two divisions. Reorganizing the armored, artillery and engineer regiments into independent brigades indicates the creation of a strategic reserve with counter attack and offensive capability. There can be two reasons for acquiring this capability.

- Bangladesh has been indulging in large scale anti-Indian activities like sheltering and aiding Indian insurgent groups on its soil, engaging in large scale illegal infiltration into Assam to finally taking over the state and helping Muslim terrorists conduct terror strikes in India. They are afraid that India could retaliate with large scale military operations against it sooner or later.
- It is developing an offensive capability of up to two divisions to attack India in association with China and annexe Assam and other north-eastern states and divide north-east India between China and itself.

Conclusions

Bangladesh was created in December 1971, when India defeated the Pakistan Army in erstwhile East Pakistan and handed over power to Sheikh Mujibur Rehman, its first Prime Minister. In spite of this, Bangladesh has been unfriendly to India during most of its 38 years of independence. As

Bangladesh had been a part of Pakistan and has a predominantly Muslim population, it draws its political and strategic ideologies from Pakistan and Saudi Arabia. Like Pakistan, Bangladesh's politics get defined in the context of anti-India stances. Like Pakistan, Bangladesh has come under growing influence of Islamic fundamentalists. During the past government of Begum Khaleda Zia, the Jammat group was part of the ruling coalition. Bangladesh shares a long and porous 3901 km border with India. This has enabled more than 2 million Bangladeshi nationals to move into India as illegal immigrants. Bangladesh offers Pakistan a fertile ground for basing its proxy war apparatus to strategically weaken India on its East and North-eastern peripheries. This arises from common religious links and shared heritage of its intelligence and military establishments with those of Pakistan. Like the Pakistan Army, the Bangladesh Army has over thrown the civilian government, ruled the country under martial law and has the final say in defence and foreign policy matters.

The Pakistan-China strategic nexus in South Asia comes into play in Bangladesh. Bangladesh is not averse to playing off Pakistan and China against India. The Bangladesh-China Defence Cooperation is a result of this geopolitical environment. The current Awami League government may be more favourably disposed towards India. But governments and policies of nations keep changing. The growing military cooperation between China and Bangladesh including the Bangladesh-China Defence Cooperation Agreement has serious strategic and tactical implications for India. The implications are discussed in detail in Chapter 10.

China's Relations with Sri Lanka

6

Background

Sri Lanka became independent of British rule as a dominion in 1948. Mr. Bandaranaike became Prime Minister in 1956 and championed Sinhalese nationalism. He made Sinhala the country's only official language, provided state support to Buddhism and marginalized the Tamil minority. He was assassinated in 1959 by a Buddhist monk. His widow, Mrs. Sirimavo Bandaranaike, became the world's first female Prime Minister in 1960. Sri Lanka's relations with India were very cordial to start with. The Tamil minority's mounting resentment toward the Sinhalese majority's monopoly on political and economic power erupted in bloody violence in 1983. Tamil rebel groups, the strongest of which were the Liberation Tigers of Tamil Eelam, or LTTE, began a civil war to fight for a separate Tamil nation or "Eelam". Relations between Sri Lanka and India soured somewhat with the rise of the ethnic conflict between the Sinhalese and the Tamil people as Sri Lanka believed that the Tamils were being aided by India in their search for "Eelam".

In July 1983, communal riots took place all over Sri Lanka due to the ambush and killing of 13 Sri Lankan Army soldiers by the Tamil Tigers. The Tamil community faced a backlash from Sinhalese rioters. Homes and shops of Tamils were burned and Tamils were assaulted. During these riots, the government did nothing to control the mobs. Around 18,000 Tamil homes and 5,000 shops were destroyed. Over 150,000

Tamils left the country creating a Tamil Diaspora in Canada, UK, Australia and other western countries. In 1987, there was an army offensive in the Jaffana peninsular which led to large scale human rights abuses against the Tamil population. India started getting deeply involved in the ethnic conflict. A naval convoy with humanitarian aid sent by India was stopped in Sri Lankan waters by the Sri Lankan Navy. The Indian Air Force retaliated with an air drop of supplies onto the Jaffna peninsula. The Sri Lankan government organized street protests against India. Prime Minister Mr. Jayawardene declared that he would defend the country's independence to the last bullet. Indo-Sri Lankan relations began to deteriorate. However, the display of Indian military power through the air drop caused Mr. Jayawardene to reconsider his position. He accepted the offer of Indian Prime Minister Rajiv Gandhi of a Peace Accord. Rajiv Gandhi sent a Peace Keeping Force (IPKF) into Sri Lanka. The move was deeply unpopular with the Sinhalese and initially popular with the Tamils. But IPKF's attempts to restrain the LTTE led to an outbreak of hostilities between the Tamil Tigers and the IPKF. This is known as Eelam War II. Indo-Sri Lankan relations reached its nadir.

In 1989, Mr. Jayawardene was succeeded by Mr. Premadasa as President of Sri Lanka. Premadasa asked for the Indian troops to be withdrawn. This was done by Indian Prime Minister Mr. V.P. Singh. Mr. Rajeev Gandhi was assassinated by a Tamil Tiger suicide bomber in 1991. This led to LTTE being declared a terrorist organization by the Indian government and banned. Relations between India and Sri Lanka began to improve.

President Premadasa was assassinated by a Tamil Tiger suicide bomber in 1992. Mrs. Kumaratunga was elected President in August, 1994. A ceasefire between Sri Lankan Army and LTTE followed. But it did not last long. The Tamil Tigers broke the ceasefire and started the Eelam War III. The Sri Lankan military was unable to defeat the separatists and the government was opposed to negotiations. By 2000, an estimated 65,000 people, mostly civilians had been killed in the conflict. Mr. Wickremasinghe became Prime Minister in December, 2001, and another cease fire began. In March,

2004, the President dismissed Mr. Wickremasinghe and called fresh elections. Mr. Mahinda Rajapaksha, the present President of Sri Lanka, thus came to power. He decided on a military solution to the ethnic problem. He left no stone unturned to strengthen the armed forces and launched an all out offensive against the LTTE in July, 2006. Thus Eelam War IV started. After about three years of bitter fighting, the Sri Lankan government declared total victory on May 18, 2009. The Sri Lankan military, thus, effectively concluded its 26 year operation against the LTTE. Sri Lankan Defence Secretary confirmed that 6,261 personnel of the Sri Lankan Armed Forces had lost their lives and 29,551 were wounded during Eelam War IV. Approximately, 22,000 LTTE cadres had died during this time. Over 60,000 civilians also died and about 1.5 million Tamil's have been rendered homeless.

Early Relations between China and Sri Lanka

Sri Lanka government recognized Peoples Republic of China in 1950. China and Sri Lanka established diplomatic relations in 1957. Premier Zhou En-lai visited Sri Lanka twice in 1957 and 1964. Sri Lanka Prime Minister Mrs. Bandaranaike visited China in 1961 and 1972. The two countries have maintained cordial relations and exchanged visits of dignitaries ever since. The Sri Lanka government has always pursued a friendly policy towards China and strongly supported China on the Taiwan and Tibet questions and human rights issue. The two countries share consensus on many major international issues and enjoy sound cooperation between them.

The Dragon Enters

Once President Rajapaksha had decided to impose a military solution to the Tamil Eelam issue, he had to find a way to strengthen the armed forces and find a way to economically sustain the conflict. India and the West were not willing to support a military solution. So, Rajapaksha turned to China and its ally, Pakistan. The Chinese government seized the opportunity with both hands and provided the Sri Lankan government arms, ammunitions, tanks, fighter planes and all military and economic assistance necessary to win the war.

China has promised continued support of the Chinese government for Sri Lanka's sovereignty, territorial integrity and President Mahinda Rajapaksa's efforts to bring about a solution to the ethnic conflict and achieve ethnic solidarity in the country through military action. This support has enabled Sri Lanka's government to jettison a five-year cease-fire in 2008 and go for an all out military action against the LTTE. Sri Lankan government ignores India's concerns about the Sri Lankan Tamils and also ignores complaints from US and European Union about human rights violations in the war. The government has lost defence aid from the United States and some other sources. But the loss has been more than made up by military aid from China and Pakistan.

In exchange for Chinese support, the Sri Lankan government agreed to the establishment of a Chinese naval base to be built on the Sri Lankan coast. China has thus been able to strengthen its position in the geopolitical struggle for power over the energy trade routes along the Indian ocean.

Economic Relations

China and Sri Lanka trade totaled US $0.34 billion in 2001 and $0.35 billion in 2006. China's exports accounted for US $0.34 billion and its imports were just US $10 million. China is increasing the volume of its investments in Sri Lanka. In 2007, Chinese assistance grew fivefold to nearly US $1 billion, surpassing Japan, formerly Sri Lanka's largest economic supporter. China has recently started explorations for oil in Sri Lanka. It is providing support for the construction of a new port and bunker facilities at Hambantota. The Hambantota Bunkering system and Tank Farm Project was undertaken by the Chinese government subsequent to a visit of Chinese Premier Wen Jiabao to Sri Lanka in April 2005. It will cost about $300 million. The project has already begun. China is also funding a coal powered power plant that will generate 20 giga watts by the year 2020. A sum of Rs. 1.5 billion (US $15m), would be invested by the Chinese Harbour Engineering Company for re-constructing six fishing harbours out of the 10 destroyed by the tsunami. This would be completed within a period of 18 months. The Chinese entrepreneurs would also get involved in the Puttalam Coal Power, the Colombo-Katunayake Expressway, Colombo-Katunayake Airport Rail link, the Phosphate Mining and NPK Compound Fertilizer Project and the Kotte Sewerage System Project.

The Sri Lankan government is likely to face economic problems and inflation is expected to reach double digits. The Western nations and UN are unhappy with Sri Lanka's human rights record. They want war crimes investigations to be carried out. Sri Lankan government has refused to do so. Its defiance of the West could cause Sri Lanka to lose trade preferences with the European Union and the US. There is no doubt that China has risen its importance for Sri Lanka. But Europe still remains the country's largest trading partner and market for its exports.

Military Cooperation

China has declared support for Sri Lankan Government in its battle against the LTTE. China came to Colombo's rescue after US stopped aid to Sri Lanka, because of its human rights violations. Sri Lanka signed a US $37.6 million classified arms deal with Chinese defence manufacturers in April 2007, to supply small arms, ammunition and equipment for its army and navy. Beijing has also roped in its ally Pakistan into providing arms to Sri Lanka. Pakistan has increased its military assistance to Sri Lanka to over $ 100 million. China sold huge quantities of arms to Sri Lanka in 2008 and boosted annual aid from $ 200 million in 2007 to $ 1 billion in 2008. China is now the largest donor to Sri Lanka. Its Jian 7 fighter jets and anti aircraft guns, JY 11-3D air surveillance radars played a key role in Sri Lanka's successes against the LTTE. Pakistan has trained the Sri Lankan air force in ground attacks and precision bombing. (*Times News Network*, April 27, 2009). It is believed that the Chinese see their stake in the Hambantota port project not only as a method to gain favour with the Sri Lankan government but also as a way to establish a strategic Chinese naval presence on the primary East-West sea trade route that lies just six nautical miles away.

The Sri Lanka Armed Forces

The total strength of the three services numbers around 230,000 active personnel. The Sri Lankan Army had a small strength of about 20,000 regular troops in 1987. The troops consisted of about two divisions with limited supporting units. By 2007, the strength had grown to about 120,000 regulars and another 30,000 reservists and paramilitary forces. The regular army now has thirteen infantry divisions divided into three operational commands. It also has an air mobile brigade, one special forces brigade, one independent armored brigade and three mechanized brigades. The deployment is given as below. (Refer Map No: 4)

The Jaffna Command consists of 51 and 52 Divisions which are deployed in the Jaffna peninsula, 53 Division, a mechanized brigade and an air mobile brigade at the Elephant Pass and 55 Division with an armored brigade also deployed at the Elephant Pass.

The Vanni Command consists of 56 Division and 61 Division at Vavunia, 57 Division with one additional brigade at Killinochi, 58 Division and a special forces brigade at Elephant Pass and 59 Division at Mullaitivu. The last three were involved in the final battle with LTTE.

The Eastern Command has three divisions. 21 and 22 Divisions are located at Trincomallee and 23 Division at Battcolaoa. The 2 and 3 Divisions are reserve divisions located at Colombo, Western and Central Sri Lanka.

The phenomenal increase in the Sri Lankan Army has been possible through Chinese arms aid and purchase of Chinese equipment. Most of the Army is equipped with Chinese equipment. Some of the equipment available with the Sri Lankan army include T55, Type 59, Type 63 Tanks, BMP1, BMP2, BMP3, Nornico Type 89, Type 93, BTR 80 and BTR 152 armored personnel carriers, 122mm, 130mm and 152mm howitzers, RM70 and BM21 multi-barrel rocket lauchers, 60mm, 82mm and 120mm mortars and Bakhtar Sikha anti-tank missiles.

Map No. 4: Map of Sri Lanka

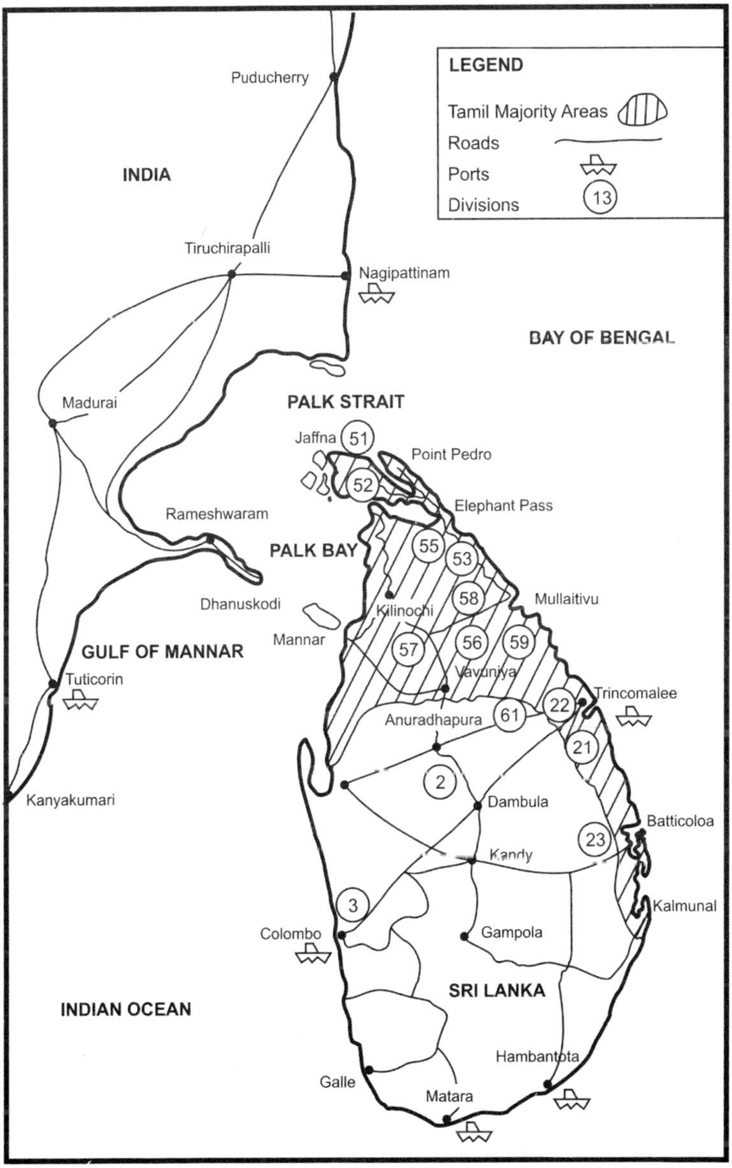

Conclusion

Cordial relations between India and Sri Lanka is impossible unless Sri Lanka is able to successfully bridge the communal divide. The Chinese want to have dominating influence in Sri Lanka due to the island's strategic location near important shipping routes. China sees these sea lanes as vital, because its energy supplies pass through the Indian Ocean region. Sri Lanka's proximity to the Indian mainland is also attractive as Chinese presence in Sri Lanka furthers its strategy of focusing on containing Indian influence. The strategy will utilize economic tools such as aid, trade and infrastructural development as well as enhanced military cooperation. The strategy will take full advantage of the Sri Lankan fears of Indian support for Sri Lankan Tamils. A hostile Sri Lanka will make it difficult for the Indian Navy to move its naval assets from the Bay of Bengal to the Arabian Sea and vice versa.

India cannot stop Sri Lanka from cozying up to the Chinese. The only way it can contain the damage is by helping create an independent Tamil home land in Sri Lanka.

China's Relations with Myanmar

7

Background

Myanmar (then Burma) gained independence on January 4, 1948. The early years of Burmese independence were marked by insurgencies by communist groups and ethnic tribes. Remote areas of Northern Myanmar were for many years controlled by an army of Nationalist Chinese forces who had fled their country in 1949 after their defeat at the hands of the Communists. Myanmar initially strove to be non-aligned in world affairs. It was one of the first countries in the world to recognize Israel and the Peoples Republic of China. By 1958, the country was beginning to fall apart politically due to a split in the ruling party. The military feared that communists would come to power. Mr. U. Nu, the first Prime Minister, invited Army Chief General Ne Win to take over the country. Communist sympathizers were purged. Ne Win's caretaker government successfully stabilized the situation. New general elections were held in 1960. U. Nu's Union Party returned with a large majority.

1962-1988

In March 1962, General Ne Win, with sixteen other senior military officers, staged a coup and declared Myanmar a socialist state. A number of protests followed the coup but they were ruthlessly suppressed by the military. All opposition parties were banned in 1964.

The Kachin Independence Organization (KIO) started an insurgency in 1961 when Prime Minister U. Nu declared Buddhism as the state religion. The Shan State Army also launched a rebellion in 1964, because of the 1962 military coup. Ne Win isolated the country from contact with the rest of the world. A one party system was established. Commerce and industry were nationalized across the board. In April 1972, General Ne Win and the rest of the Revolutionary Council retired from the military but continued to run the country. A new constitution was promulgated in January 1974 that resulted in the creation of a People's Assembly that held supreme legislative, executive, and judicial authority. Ne Win became the President of the new government.

In 1978, a military operation was conducted against the Rohingiya Muslims in Arakan region bordering Bangladesh. This resulted in about 250,000 refugees fleeing to neighboring Bangladesh. Mr. U. Nu was released from prison in October 1966. He left Burma in April 1969 and formed the Parliamentary Democracy Party (PDP) in Bangkok. The PDP launched an armed rebellion across the Thai border from 1972 till 1978 but failed to gain power. U. Nu and his comrades returned to Rangoon after being granted amnesty. In the 1980s, there was an economic crisis. This led to economic reforms in 1987-88 that relaxed socialist controls and encouraged foreign investment. This was not enough, to stop growing economic turmoil in the country. Ne Win retired as President in 1981.

1988-2008

The period of 1980s saw widespread protests and demonstrations throughout the country. The military responded by firing on the crowds, alleging Communist infiltration. Violence, chaos and anarchy reigned. The armed forces staged another coup on September 18, 1988 to restore order. The military killed thousands, abolished the 1974 Constitution and imposed martial law. The Army claimed that the uprising had been orchestrated by the Communist Party of Burma (CPB) through its underground organizations. The Communist leaders were soon forced into exile across the Chinese border.

The military government announced a change of name for the country from Burma to Myanmar in 1989. It also continued the economic reforms started by the old regime and called for a Constituent Assembly to revise the 1974

Constitution. This led to multi-party elections in May 1990 in which the National League for Democracy (NLD) won a landslide victory. The military government, however, did not let the assembly convene. It placed the leader of the NLD, Aung San Suu Kyi under house arrest. Burma came under increasing international pressure to convene the elected assembly, particularly after Aung San Suu Kyi was awarded the Nobel Peace Prize in 1991.

The Military Junta finally allowed a National convention to meet in 1993 to review the constitution but insisted that the assembly preserve a major role for the military in any future government. The NLD was not ready to accept the condition and walked out. The government reconvened the National Convention in 1995 in an attempt to rewrite the Constitution. The Military Junta relaxed some of the restrictions on Aung San Suu Kyi's house arrest and finally released her in 1995. She was forbidden to leave Yangon. However, major pro-democracy organizations and parties, including the NLD, were barred from participating. The military allowed only selected smaller parties to participate. But a new constitution could not be agreed upon. The assembly was finally dismissed in March 1996 without producing a constitution.

During the 1990s, the military regime had to deal with several insurgencies by tribal minorities along its borders. The regime was able to negotiate cease-fire agreements that ended the fighting with the hill tribes such as the Wa and the Kachins, but the Karens did not negotiate. The military finally captured the main Karen base in 1995, but no final peace settlement with the Karens has been finalized. Khan Sa, a major opium warlord who nominally controlled parts of Shan state, made a deal with the government in December 1995 after U.S. pressure.

The military mounted two major crackdowns on the NLD in 1996 and 1997. Continuing reports of human rights violations in Burma led the US to intensify sanctions in 1997. The European Union followed suit in 2000. The military placed Aung San Suu Kyi under house arrest again. She remains under house arrest even today. The government also carried out another large scale crackdown on the NLD, arrested many of its leaders and closed down most of its offices. The capital city was relocated from Yangon to Navpyidaw in January 2006.

In 2007, the Military Junta removed fuel subsidies which caused the price of diesel and petrol to suddenly rise as much as 100 per cent. This led to large scale protests. The protest demonstrations were dealt with quickly and harshly by the Military Junta. Hundreds of protesters were arrested and detained. Buddhist monks took part in the protests and were brutally suppressed. On February 7, 2008, the Junta announced that a referendum for the Constitution would be held by 2010 and elections would follow. The referendum was held on May 10, 2008 and promised a "discipline-flourishing democracy" for the country in the future. The promised elections are yet to be held. The Military Junta has ruled Myanmar since 1988. The situation in Burma remains tense to this day.

China-Myanmar Relations

Background

Burma was the first non-Communist country to recognize the Communist-led People's Republic of China after its formation in 1949. Burma and the People's Republic of China formally established diplomatic relations on June 8, 1950. China and Burma signed a treaty of friendship and mutual non-aggression and promulgated a Joint Declaration on June 29, 1954. Beijing had always identified Burma as vital to the well-being of its impoverished provinces in the south-west, Yunnan, Sichuan and Guizhou.

The relations between the two countries turned hostile in the sixties. The Communist Party of Burma (CPB) had fled to China in face of persecution by the military and had received support at the hands of the Communist government in China. There were anti-Chinese riots in 1967 and the Chinese communities were expelled from Burma.

Relations began to improve significantly in the 1970s. Under the rule of Deng Xiaoping, China reduced support for the CPB. In 1988, the Military Junta under the title of "State Peace and Development Council" (SPDC) assumed power and carried out violent repression against pro-democracy agitators. This resulted in growing international condemnation and pressure. The Military Junta found it necessary to cultivate a strong relationship with China to survive. China signed a major trade agreement with Burma, legalized cross-border trade and began supplying large quantities of military aid. Thus China's influence grew rapidly after the international community abandoned Burma. China and Russia has vetoed an UN Security Council resolution designed to punish Burma and may do so in the future.

At the outset of the twenty first century, the overriding goal of the Burmese Military Junta is the survival of its regime. Close and cordial relations with China are a key element of the strategy. As such, the two countries regularly exchange high-level visits. Domestic developments in Myanmar in 2003 and 2004 helped to further strengthen Sino-Myanmar relations. Following the attacks on Aung San Suu Kyi's entourage by pro-SPDC militias on May 30, 2003, the United States, EU and Japan tightened sanctions against Burma. This has increased Myanmar's reliance on China for economic sustenance. The downfall of Prime Minister Khin Nyunt in October 2004, who is widely regarded as the architect of Sino-Myanmar relations, was initially seen as a blow for China, especially when SPDC Chairman General Than Shwe paid a state visit to India just a week later. Nevertheless, within days of Khin Nyunt's ouster, his successor, Lieutenant General Soe Win was in Beijing, followed by Lieutenant General Thura Shwe Mann, Than Shwe's heir apparent. These visits were no doubt intended to reassure Beijing that the SPDC still valued China as its most important ally. Beijing has occasionally expressed concern over the complete lack of progress toward political reform in Burma, principally because of its potential for social and political unrest. In 2004, Premier Wen Jiabao stated that, while the political process was Burma's internal affair, the Chinese government hoped the SPDC would speed-up "political settlements of existing disputes so as to enhance stability and peaceful development".

Economic Relations

Myanmar has very strong economic relations with China. It would not be wrong to say that in the regime of sanctions by US and the European Union, its economic survival depends on Chinese economic support. China has provided soft loans to the military regime as well as economic aid and investments for the construction of dams, bridges, roads, ports and industrial projects. To exploit the river and road networks in Myanmar, China has entered into a long-term agreement with Myanmar. China is building new roads linking Myanmar with the South-West provinces, clearing the Irrawady river for bigger barges and modernizing some of the ports and shipyards of Myanmar. China extensively financed the construction of strategic roads along the Irrawaddy River trade route linking China's Yunnan province to the Bay of Bengal.

Myanmar is an important element in China's quest for energy security. It has received the rights to develop and exploit natural gas reserves in the Arakan region. Chinese firms have been involved in the construction of oil and gas pipelines stretching 2,380 km from Burma's Arakan coast to China's Yunnan Province. Petro China is in the process of building a major gas pipeline from the A-1 Shwe oil field, off the coast of Myanmar, to Yunnan, accessing and exploiting an estimated 2.88 to 3.56 trillion cubic feet of natural gas (Refer Map No: 5). A proposed Sino-Myanmar oil pipeline off the western coast of Burma may permit China to import oil from the Middle East bypassing the Straits of Malacca.

Beijing continues to dole out soft loans to the Myanmar government. For instance, in 2003, China helped stabilize the economy after a banking crisis with $200 million in preferential loans and partial debt relief on earlier loans (*Financial Times*, January 17, 2003). China has maintained its position as Myanmar's top trade and investment partner. In 2005, bilateral trade hit $1.21 billion, much of it in China's favor; China exported $935 million worth of goods to Myanmar, but only imported $274 million (*People's Daily*, July 31, 2006). Bilateral trade between China and Myanmar exceeded $1.4 billion in 2008.

Military Relations

China has extensive strategic and military cooperation with Myanmar. It is the most important supplier of military aid to Myanmar's Military Junta since its takeover of the power in 1988 and has supplied more than $3 billions worth of arms since 1989. China has supplied Myanmar with jet fighters, armored vehicles and naval vessels. It has trained Burmese army, navy and air force personnel. In return, China has been granted access to Burma's ports and naval installations. This has enabled China to increase its strategic influence in the Bay of Bengal and the Indian Ocean. China has developed a deep-water port at Kyaukpvu in the Bay of Bengal. It has also built a jetty, naval facilities and installed reconnaissance and electronic intelligence systems on the Great Coco Island which is located only 18 km from India's Andaman and Nicobar Islands. This base gives China the capabilities to monitor India's military activities in the Bay of Bengal, including missile tests. China is assisting in constructing a naval base at Sittwe, a strategically important sea port. China is also helping Myanmar in modernizing its naval bases at Hanggyi, Akyab and Mergui. Beijing has also funded road construction linking Yangon and Sittwe, providing the shortest route to the Indian Ocean from southern China.

Myanmar's Relations with India and other Nations

Despite close links with Beijing, the SPDC continues to diversify its foreign relations. In recent years, Myanmar has shown an willingness to develop strategic and commercial relations with India. Once New Delhi committed itself to a policy of remaining silent on the political situation in Myanmar, relations with the SPDC improved rapidly. In November 2000, General Maung Aye, the second highest ranking member of the SPDC hierarchy visited New Delhi to discuss trade, transport links, counter-insurgency cooperation and arms procurement. Since then the two countries have exchanged high-level visits, including a visit by Indian President A.P.J. Abdul Kalam in March 2006. India has supplied the Myanmar Army with tanks, artillery and helicopters. The two countries' armed forces have conducted coordinated military operations against Indian insurgents. India has built a highway connecting Manipur with Myanmar's road system. New Delhi is trying to get into exploiting Myanmar's energy resources. Myanmar's trade and military cooperation with India has increased. It could mean a shift in Myanmar's foreign policy to avoid excessive dependence on China.

Map No. 5: Map of Myanmar

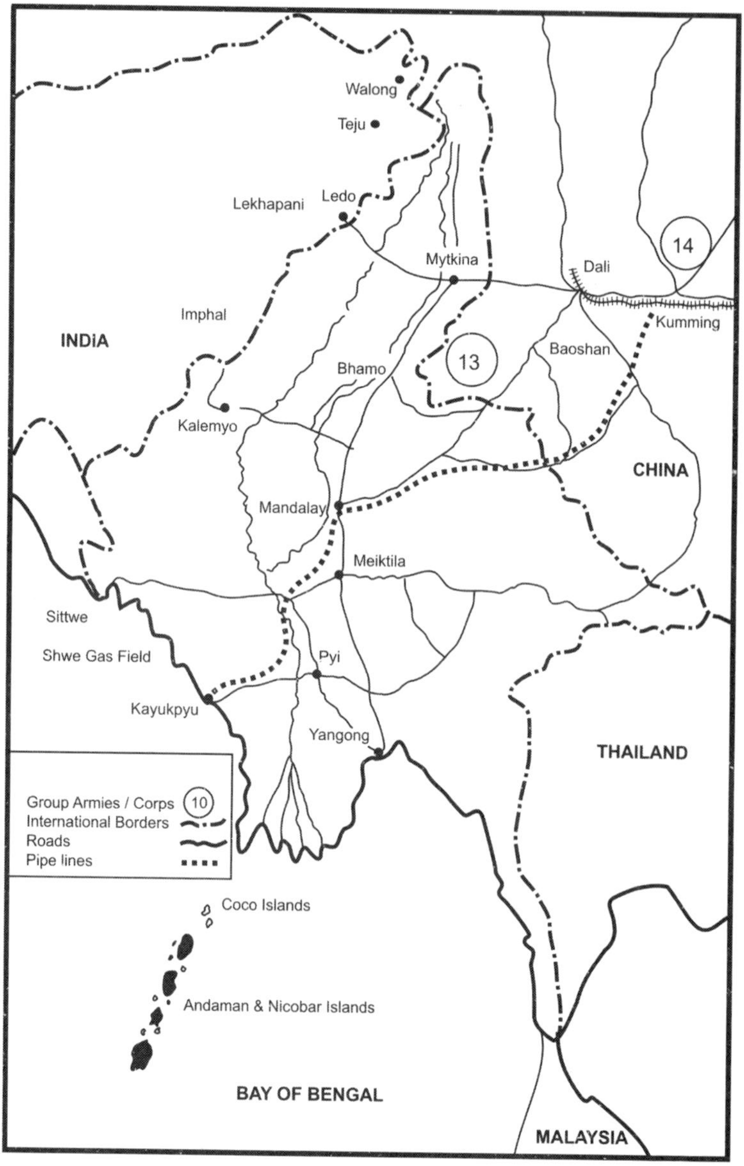

Since 2000, Myanmar has also allowed itself to be courted by Russia. Enhanced relations with Moscow have provided the SPDC with several benefits, including an alternative source of arms. Moscow has agreed to provide Myanmar with MiG-29 fighters and air defence systems and invest in the country's energy sector. Russian interest in Burma was demonstrated in January 2007 when Russia vetoed a US proposal for sanctions against Myanmar at the UN Security Council. China is reportedly unhappy with the SPDC's courtship of India and Russia.

Myanmar's Armed Forces

The Myanmar Army

The Myanmar Army has always been by far the largest Service of Myanmar's armed forces and has always received the lion's share of Myanmar's defence budget. It has a strength of about 400,000 and about 800 tanks. It has been at the forefront of Myanmar's battle against the numerous tribal insurgent groups fighting for independence or autonomy since 1948. Myanmar's infantry is rated by some as the toughest and most seasoned in Southeast Asia.

The army is organized into Light Infantry Divisions, Regional Operation Commands (ROCs) and Military Operation Commands (MOCs). ROCs and MOCs have been stationed in insurgency affected tribal areas (Karen State, Kachin State, United Wa State, Shan State on Thailand Myanmar Border, Kokang rebel area, and eastern Shan State) where ceasefire agreement is in operation with 17 armed ethnic groups since 1990. Each ROC deploys at least five battalions in the ethnic area it controls. The ROC commander exercises financial, administrative and judicial authority in his area. MOCs were formed in 1995. They are also stationed in tribal areas. MOCs are located in northern Shan State, southern Shan State, Kachin State, Karen State and Mon State. MOCs were formed to organize military activities in these areas more efficiently. The MOC is equivalent to the Light Infantry Division. Both have ten infantry battalions with a brigadier-general as commander. By 2008, the Myanmar Army had 504 infantry battalions under thirteen ROCs, ten Light Infantry Divisions and twenty MOCs.

Myanmar Air Force

The Myanmar Air Force was formed on December 24, 1947. It is the youngest and smallest element of Myanmar's armed forces. It has a strength of about 10,000. It has about 125 aircraft of various types including about 2 squadrons of Chinese F-7 Fighters, a squadron of Indian helicopters and Russian MiG 29s.

Myanmar Navy

The Myanmar Navy has a strength of about 19,000. It was formed in 1940 and, although very small, played an active part in Allied operations against the Japanese during the Second World War. The Myanmar Navy currently operates more than 122 vessels including four frigates. The navy has always been an important factor in Myanmar's security. It was dramatically expanded in recent years to provide a blue water capability. It has two naval infantry battalions.

Defence Production

The Myanmar defence industries consist of 13 major factories throughout the country that produce approximately 70 major products for Army, Navy and Air Force. The main products include automatic rifles, machine guns, anti-aircraft guns, complete range of mortar and artillery ammunition, aircraft and anti-aircraft ammunition, tank and anti-tank ammunition, anti-tank and anti-personal mines. Myanmar's defence industries are said to be the most modern defence industry in the south-east Asia region. China is the main source of technology. Vital components for Myanmar's infantry fighting vehicle such as fire control systems, turrets, engines and transmissions are imported from China's NORINCO industries. Production facility for the BTR-3U wheeled armored personnel carrier has been established with Ukrainian assistance. Approximately, 1,000 BTR-3U wheeled APCs are to be assembled in Myanmar over the next 10 years. Myanmar is also producing a number of military trucks and jeeps for the Army, Navy and Air Force.

Conclusion

As long as the Military Junta (SPDC) remains in power, Beijing will retain its position as Myanmar's primary patron.

China's veto power at the UN and financial clout makes it a far more valuable ally than India. There is also a fear that future Indian governments might yet put pressure on Myanmar to democratize. Should relations with India sour over human rights issues, Burma's dependence on China would only increase. Moreover, this dependence would deepen if Myanmar's relations with ASEAN became more strained and Burma's membership was suspended or forfeited.

However, things may change. The Military Junta may be forced to relinquish power as the result of a popular uprising, leading to the restoration of democracy. A democratic Burma, possibly led by Aung San Suu Kyi, would most likely orient the country's foreign policy toward the West, India and Japan. This would be a major setback for China's interests in south-east Asia. Beijing would lose a pliant friend and all the economic and geo-strategic advantages it has gained since 1988. In order to forestall such an outcome, Beijing may be tempted to intervene militarily in support of the SPDC. In fact, China has permanently deployed a Category A Army Group on Myanmar border just for such an eventuality.

A third scenario is also possible. A major nationalist backlash against China could occur at some stage, because of the Chinese domination of upper Myanmar or northern Myanmar. There is a growing resentment in the area, because of income disparities between impoverished Burmese and well to do Chinese immigrants. A xenophobic outburst of this nature is not without precedent. In 1964, the Myanmar government expelled hundreds of thousands of Indians (who made up the bulk of the commercial class) from the country. In 1967, violent anti-Chinese riots took place in Yangon. Such a backlash could strain the Sino-Myanmar alliance to a breaking point.

As things stand today, with the tightening of US and EU sanctions, and as ASEAN's patience with the generals wears thin, the first scenario remains the most probable. If China uses northern Myanmar to attack India, it is unlikely that the Military Junta will do anything to stop it.

China's Relations with Nepal

8

Background

Modern Nepal was created in the 18th Century when Prithvi Narrayan Shah unified the country under his rule and established the Shah Dynasty. Between 1788 and 1791, Nepal invaded Tibet and plundered the Tashilhunpo Monastery at Sighaste. The Chinese emperor responded by dispatching a sizeable army that defeated the Nepalese army. Nepal and the British in India fought the Anglo-Nepalese War from 1814 to 1816. Nepal was soundly defeated and had to sign the Treaty of Sugauli in 1816, ceding the Nepali territories of Terrai and Sikkim to the British. In exchange Nepal was not annexed by the British. Terrai became a part of India. Sikkim was later annexed by India. In 1846, a military leader of Indian ancestry overthrew the Shah Dynasty and established the Rana Dynasty of hereditary prime ministers. The Shah Dynasty remained titular rulers. The Ranas were staunchly pro-British and assisted the British during the Sepoy Mutiny of 1857.

The Indian struggle for independence inspired the Nepalese leaders to demand democracy. The turmoil culminated in King Tribhuvan fleeing from house arrest to India in 1950. The King signed the 1950 Indo-Nepal Treaty of Peace and Friendship that established a close Indo-Nepalese relationship on commerce, defence and foreign relations. India in return helped to restore the monarchy. The Treaty was resented by some political parties of Nepal. Many in Nepal saw it as an encroachment of its sovereignty and an unwelcome extension of Indian influence. The deployment of an Indian military mission in Nepal in the 1950s increased these concerns.

In 1959, Tribhuvan's son King Mahendra issued a new constitution in an attempt to control the pro-democracy movement. The first democratic elections for a national assembly were held in 1960. The Nepali Congress Party gained a substantial victory in the election. Its leader, B.P. Koirala formed a government and served as Prime Minister. However, the democratic government was short lived. In 1962, King Mahendra declared parliamentary democracy as a failure. He dismissed the elected Koirala government and declared that a partyless "panchayat" system would govern Nepal. He promulgated a new constitution. The elected Prime Minister, Members of Parliament and hundreds of activists supporting democracy were arrested. This trend of arrest of political activists and democracy supporters continued for the entire 30 year period of partyless "panchayati" system under King Mahendra and then his son, King Birendra. In 1979, King Birendra called for a national referendum to decide on the nature of Nepal's government. The referendum was held in May 1980. The "panchayat" system won a narrow victory. The king carried out the promised reforms including selection of the Prime Minister by the Rastriya Panchayat. There was relative peace till a dispute with India led to India's closing of most border crossings between India and Nepal from March 1989 to July 1990. In 1990, the Nepali Congress along with leftist parties decided to launch a decisive movement for multi-party parliamentary democracy. The movement forced the monarchy to accept constitutional reforms and to establish a multi-party parliament. In May 1991, Nepal held its first parliamentary elections in nearly 30 years. The Nepali Congress won 110 of the 205 seats and formed the first elected government in 32 years. Mid-term elections in November 1994, which were called after the government lost a parliamentary vote, resulted in a hung parliament and the communists, who emerged as the single largest party, formed a minority government.

Inadequate development of rural Nepal led to a Maoist insurgency in 1996. The civil war between Maoists and the Nepalese government began in 1996. Most of the fighting has occurred in rural areas and in the western districts. The army was called in and began actively engaging the Maoists in 2001. Peace talks in 2001 and 2003 were unsuccessful. By 2005, the Maoists had control over an estimated 40 to 60 per cent of the country. Independent observers contend that a significant portion of the rural population was supportive of the insurgents' goals. But they were fed up with repressive activities of both the Maoists and the government. It is believed that from February 13, 1996, to September 16, 2005, about 13,000 persons were killed in the conflict and over 50,000 persons were displaced. King Birendra was assassinated in 2004 and his brother Gyanendra became king. King Gyanendra dissolved the Parliament in 2005 and assumed direct rule to suppress the Maoist insurgency. In 2006, anti-monarchy pro-democracy forces and Maoists came together. Maoists came over ground. King Gyanendra was forced to abdicate and the monarchy was dissolved in 2008.

After the peace process and national elections in Nepal in 2008, a new Maoist led government came to power through a coalition. The Maoists had announced their intentions to renegotiate Nepal's 1950 treaty with India. But the Maoist Prime Minister and Nepal's President fell out over the sacking of the Army Chief by the government in 2009 over his objection to induction of Maoist cadres into the Army. The issue has been resolved for the time being and a new government has assumed office under a new prime minister. Nepal has a difficult task balancing its relations with China and India.

Nepal's Relations with China

Nepal invaded Tibet, then a part of China, for the second time in 1854. China intervened and defeated the Nepalese. The Treaty of Thapathali was signed between the two in March 1856. The treaty recognized China's suzerainty over Tibet and Nepal agreed to pay annual feudatory tribute. Relations between Nepal and China and Tibet continued without any major incident until 1904, when British India sent an armed expedition to Tibet. Nepal rejected Tibet's request for aid to avoid British reprisal. Beginning 1908, Nepal stopped paying tribute to China. In 1910, China reasserted its claim to sovereign rights in Tibet and feudatory tributes from Nepal. Nepal broke relations with China when the Tibetans, taking advantage of the Chinese revolution of 1911, drove the Chinese out.

China occupied Tibet in 1950 and imposed restrictions on Nepalese contacts with Tibet. China also increased its support for the Communist Party of Nepal, which was opposed to the Nepalese Monarchy. The break in diplomatic relations between Kathmandu and Beijing continued until 1955, when relations were re-established. The two countries exchanged ambassadors in July 1960. In 1956, both nations signed a new treaty terminating the Treaty of Thapathali of 1856. Nepal recognized Tibet as a part of China but payment of tribute stopped. In 1961, Nepal and China signed a boundary settlement agreement and a separate treaty of peace and friendship. Nepal also began supporting Communist China's bid for membership in the UN Security Council. In 1961, Nepal and China agreed to build an all-weather road connecting the Nepalese capital Kathmandu with Tibet. The highway is of immense strategic military importance to China. The highway established direct links between Nepal and two major Chinese army bases at Gyriong in Tibet. Nepal remained neutral during the Sino Indian War of 1962. In the 1970s, King Birendra proposed Nepal as a "zone of peace" between India and China. In 1974, the Nepalese Army was mobilized to disarm the Tibetan Khampas who had been using Nepalese soil to engage in a guerrilla war against the Chinese forces in Tibet. The Khampas had secretly created their base in Mustang (north-west Nepal) and were operating from there. Nepal, under immerse diplomatic pressure from China, moved nine infantry units towards the Khampa post in Mustang and forced them to surrender. Chinese leader Deng Xiaoping visited Kathmandu in February 1977.

Sino-Nepalese relations received a major fillip in 2004 when King Gyanendra took over absolute power. From 2004 to 2006, the US, UK and India refused to supply arms to the regime of King Gyanendra alleging human rights violations. China responded by dispatching arms to Nepal. The military relations and economic cooperation between China and Nepal have been improving ever since. Many Army Chiefs and Defence Secretaries of Nepal have visited China. The Defence Minister and the Chief of Staff of China have also visited Nepal. China has also assisted Nepal in the economic field. Chinese Government has appreciated Nepal government's support for the one China policy with regard to Tibet and Taiwan. Nepal's Maoist led government has recently cracked down on Tibetans, who were demonstrating against China.

China is set to bolster ties with the Maoist led government in Nepal with a massive $100 million financial aid. China has pledged that it will never change its friendly policy towards Nepal irrespective of changes both internationally and in the two countries.

Economic Relations

The bilateral economic and trade relations between Nepal and China have been increasing. The two governments agreed to set up an Economic and Trade Joint Committee between the People's Republic of China and His Majesty's Government of Nepal in 1983. In 2001, the two countries signed the Memorandum of Understanding on Tourism Cooperation. They also signed an "Air Service Agreement", according to which, Air China and Nepal airlines opened a direct air link between China and Nepal in 2004.

Nepal's total volume of trade with China was US $157 million in 2003/2004. It reached US $268 million in 2006. During the bilateral visits in 2006, the Chinese government had announced a grant of RMB120 million and concessional loan of US $200 million to Nepal.

In 2004, the total number of Chinese investment projects reached 30 with capital input of nearly US $40 million. In 2007-08, China began construction of a 770 km railway line connecting Lhasa with the Nepalese border town of Khasa. Until now, the Chinese Government has assisted Nepal to undertake many projects. These include about 400 km of highways, Seti River bridge at Pokhara, seven industrial projects, Sunkoshi Hydroelectric Project, Pokhara Water Conservancy and Irrigation Project and a number of education and healthcare projects.

Strategic relations

China has been trying to reduce Indian influence on the Nepalese Army. In the 1980s, Nepal imported Chinese weaponry in contravention of its 1950 treaty with India. Since 1998, the Nepalese Army has sent officers and soldiers to study in Chinese military universities. In the academic year of 2006/2007, 21 officers and soldiers of the Nepalese Army went to China for training. China has also sent military officers to participate in the adventure trainings organized by the Nepalese Army since 2002. China will provide 62.5 million rupees as military aid to Nepal. An agreement to this effect was signed by Defence Minister during his recent visit to China in 2008. China provided Nepal with 100 armored personnel carriers (APC) and a large number of Type 56 and Type 60 air defence guns. Nepal in turn has assured China that it will not allow its soil to be used for any activity directed against its communist neighbor.

Nepal's Relations with Pakistan and Others

Nepal established diplomatic relations with India in 1947, but did not do so with Pakistan. Nepal and Pakistan established diplomatic relations in 1962 and set up embassies in 1963. Both nations also signed agreements to grant "Most Favored Nation Status" for developing trade and cooperation. In 1963, Pakistan agreed to provide Nepal with free trade access and transport facilities through the port of Chittagong in East Pakistan (Now Bangladesh) and established an air link. This arrangement reduced Nepal's dependence on India for trading privileges. Nepal maintained neutrality during the Indo-Pak wars. It was one of the first to recognize the independence of Bangladesh. In recent years, both countries have begun developing military cooperation. Nepal has started importing arms from Pakistan. Condemned and isolated by India, UK and US between 2004 and 2006 for repressing democracy, the Nepalese monarchy developed military cooperation with China and Pakistan. The volume of bilateral trade remains comparatively small at $4.8 million despite an extensive 1982 trade agreement. Pakistan has also offered a USD 5 million line of credit to Nepal. There are allegations that Nepalese territory is being used as a haven by Islamic militants supported by Pakistan and Al Qaeda for operations against India.

Nepal also has cordial relations with the US, UK and Russia. It bought BTR 70 APCs from Russia.

Nepalese Armed Forces

Strength and Organization

Nepal has an army but no navy, coast guard, marines or air force. The Nepalese Army was reorganized into divisions in 2001. There was considerable expansion in the period 2004-06 to fight the Maoist rebels. Nepal has six combat divisions, each responsible for a particular area (Far West, Mid West, Western, Central, Eastern Nepal and the Valley). Each division includes combat brigades and combat service support units. One combat brigade is designated as the Royal Guards Brigade and there are separate army aviation, paratrooper and special operations brigades. Each brigade contains two to three infantry battalions and support units such as air defence, artillery, engineers, etc. It is estimated that in 2003 the army had about 85,000 active-duty personnel, including nearly 320 personnel in the Royal Nepal Army Air Wing. The army has no reserve component. The defence budget was approximately US $150 million for FY2006. The Indian army has 40,000 Nepalese in its Gurkha regiments. As of January 2005, Nepal was the world's fourth largest contributor of troops to UN peacekeeping missions with 3,016 troops serving in various international peacekeeping operations.

Beijing is also said to have shown interest in helping with the integration of the Maoists' guerrilla army with the

Nepalese Army. The integration remains a contentious issue. In 2006, Nepal's ruling parties had agreed to the Maoist demand that the merger would take place once the rebels laid down arms. Now there is both covert and open opposition by some of the very parties that had earlier agreed to it. Besides China, the US and UN have expressed willingness to assist with the reintegration. The offer has so far been rejected by Nepal. The integration presently stands rejected by Nepal's Army Chief who has the support of the country's president.

Major Military Equipment

The army is believed to have a mix of weapon systems from India, China, UK, Pakistan and Russia. The equipment includes armored personnel carriers, 75 mm, 94 mm and 105 mm artillery guns, 120 mm mortars, PRC Type 56 14.5-millimeter light anti-aircraft guns, 37 mm and 40 mm anti-aircraft guns. The air wing has a few 748 transport aircraft and helicopters but no combat aircraft or armed helicopters.

A high-level military delegation headed by the deputy chief of China's People's Liberation Army met Nepal's new Maoist Defence Minister in December 2008, to sign a $2.6 million military aid pact. In January 2008, the chief of Nepalese Army, visited Beijing when Chinese Defence Minister had offered assistance of 8 million yuan (about $1.1 million) that was to have comprised non-lethal military hardware. Beijing also pledged an additional security assistance of 10 million yuan (about $1.4 million). Besides the assistance, China is also interested in holding joint military training with the Nepalese Army. Nepal, on its part, has sought China's help to regulate its open northern border with Tibet.

Conclusion

The keystone of Nepal's China policy has been maintaining equal distance with China and India while simultaneously seeking to decrease India's influence and Nepal's dependence on India. Further, Kathmandu seems to believe that the competition between its two giant neighbors, China and India, would benefit its own economic development.

Nepal continues to be politically unstable. Chinese and Pakistani influence in Nepal has been increasing primarily at China's behest. India seems unable to match Chinese aid to Nepal. Chinese Army has an easy access to India through Nepal. One does not know whether such a move will be resisted by the Nepalese Army. Like all of India's neighbours, Nepal is more of a problem than an asset.

China's Build-up in Tibet

9

Background

Tibet Autonomous Region (TAR) and the Xinjiang Province of China are sensitive regions. Tibetans and the Uighur Muslims of Xinjiang have secessionist ambitions and have a history of violent protests. American presence in Afghanistan, Tibetan refugees and Dalai Lama's presence in India, presence of Taliban and Al Qaeda on China's western borders only makes the situation worse. Tibet has a 1400 km border with Nepal. China has been consolidating its relationships with the Nepalese government. China asked Nepal to close down the Tibetan Refugee Welfare Office in January 2005. China therefore maintains a large military force in the region. It has developed the capability to quickly induct troops by road, railway and air from military bases anywhere in China. Lhasa is virtually surrounded by military camps and the inner city has a heavy presence of special armed police and under-cover security personnel.

Chinese military presence in Tibet has grave strategic implications for India. China has occupied Aksai Chin area of Ladakh and claims most of Arunachal Pradesh. If China ever decides to annex Arunachal by force, it will have to use Tibet and Myanmar as launch pad for a multi-pronged offensive into India. It is therefore necessary for all Indians, particularly our political leaders, security advisers and media to be aware of China's military capabilities in Tibet and Xinjiang. Any Indian offensive into Tibet is not going to hurt mainland China. But any major Chinese offensive against India can only be launched through Tibet and Myanmar.

Infrastructure Development in Tibet

Road Network (Ref Map No: 6)

China has been improving the connectivity between main land China and Tibet ever since it annexed Tibet in 1950. By the end of 2003, some 41,302 km of roads had been completed. To date, the region has five national-level, 14 regional level and six lateral or inter connecting highways, which basically satisfy the social and economic development needs of Tibet. In addition to the 3,200 km of asphalted roads, 32,195 km of rural roads have also been built, linking some 683 townships and 5,956 villages across the region. These have been a boon for travelers and bus companies who today serve 627 townships and 4,214 villages. It has also built five network of roads leading to its borders with India and Nepal.

The Western Highway or the Xinjiang-Tibet Highway starts at Amdo and passes through Silling-Aksai Chin and connects Tibet with Xinjiang Province's road network at Mazar.

Qinghai-Tibet Highway is Tibet's longest asphalt paved road. It stretches from Xinning, the capital city of Qinghai Province to Lhasa. It has gradual gradients and is of high quality. It is the safest road to Tibet.

Sichuan-Tibet Highway runs between Chengdu, the capital city of Sichuan Province and Lhasa. Sichuan-Tibet Highway is probably the most dangerous highway in the world. It has two branches. The North Route is about 2,400 km long and the South Route of about 2,100 km. It runs across a variety of rivers and mountains with the highest point over 5,000 m above sea level. Landslides are frequent. The road is very susceptible to attack by the Indian Air Force or disruption by Tibetan resistance.

The Yunnan-Tibet Highway connects Yunnan Province to Tibet. It skirts Arunachal Pradesh from the East and will be used if China decides to attack Lohit or Subansari districts of

Arunachal Pradesh or for moving troops from Yunnan Province to Tibet.

The Sino-Nepal Highway is the only international highway in Tibet. It connects Lhasa to Kathmandu. Most of the highways in the Tibet region will be within striking range of the Su-30MKI fighters when deployed by India. If China were to have a military confrontation with India, highway transport could be more reliable than the Qinghai-Tibet railway which could be more easily damaged and difficult to repair.

Rail Network

The Qinghai-Tibet railway is the longest and highest plateau based railroad in the world. It has a total length of 1,956 km and connects Xining in Qinghai Province and Lhasa in the Tibet Autonomous Region. It was completed in 2006. The "Tibet Railway" refers to the section from Golmud to Lhasa and runs for 1,142 km and passes through mostly uninhabited zones. The Tibet Railway itself with 675 bridges is a marvel to behold. The main stations on the line are Xining, Delinga, Golmud, Amdo, Nakchu, Damxung, Lhasa. There are plans to extend the railway line from Lhasa to Kathmandu. This will indeed have geopolitical ramifications for India. China claims that the annual transport capacity of the railway was 5 million tons per year or about 14,000 tons per day. The Golmud-Lhasa pipeline has a capacity of half a million tones of fuel annually. With the completion of the Qinghai-Tibet railway line, China will be able to overcome a major obstacle to increasing its military deployment near the India-Tibet border region. Some consider that the rail link gives China the capability to induct up to 12 divisions a month into Tibet.

Airfields

Tibet has 25 airfields and air strips. All the airfields in Tibet have been lengthened and upgraded. Many air bases have been built. Currently only four are in active use but others can be activated in a short period of time.

Map No. 6: Chinese Army in Tibet

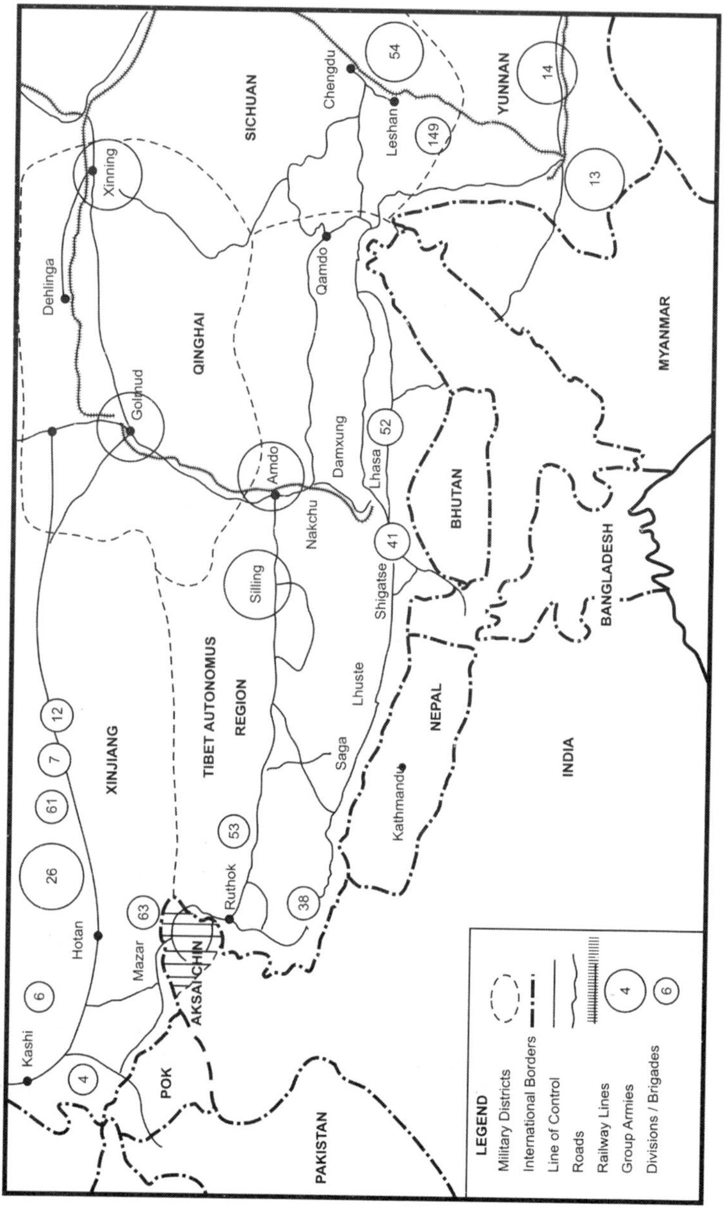

Military Build-up on the Tibetan Plateau

As we have seen in Chapter 3, China has seven Military Regions. The whole of Tibet has been put under two military regions, the Chengdu Military Region with its headquarters at Chengdu and the Lanzhou Military Region with its headquarters at Lanzhou. (See Map 2). Chengdu Military region is responsible for Tibet Autonomous Region or TAR and Sichuan and Yunnan Provinces. Lanzhou Military Region is responsible for operations in Xinjiang Province, Aksai Chin and Qinghai Province. The responsibilities of the two Military Regions are shown on Map No: 6. The strength of Chinese military personnel in Tibet is estimated to be around 500,000.

The Chengdu Military Region consists of three Group Armies (the 13th, 14th and 54th), the Tibetan 52nd and 53rd Mountain Brigades, the 149th Motorised Infantry Division at Leshan, Sichuan, two Motorised Armed Police Divisions (38th and 41st), and the 2nd Army Aviation Regiment at Chengdu. The No. 52 Brigade, stationed at Linzhi, is highly mechanized and armed with T-92 wheeled armored vehicles and HJ-8/9 anti-tank missiles. The No. 53 Mountain Brigade is stationed at Milin and is also the PLA combat unit stationed closest to the city of Lhasa.

There are six sub-military districts in the TAR. TAR is estimated to have two independent infantry brigades (Tibetan 52nd and 53rd Mountain Brigades), six border defence regiments, five independent border defence battalions, three artillery regiments, three engineers' regiments, one main signal station and two signal regiments, three transport regiments and three independent transport battalions, four air force bases, two radar regiments, and a regiment of para-military forces. It also has two division (38th and 41st) and six independent regiments of People's Armed Police. In addition, there are 12 units of what is known as the "second artillery (or the strategic nuclear missile) division". The People's Armed Police are regular PLA troops re-designated as such recently. The front line troop concentrations in the TAR are said to be located at Ruthok, Gyamuk, Drongpa, Saga, Drangso (Dhingri), Gampa-la, Dromo, Tsona, Lhuntse Dzong, Zayul, etc. close to the

LAC. The second line of defences are concentrated at Shigatse, Lhasa, Nagchukha, Tsethang, Nangartse, Gyamdha, Nyingtri, Powo Tramo, Tsawa Pomdha, Chamdo, etc. In addition, China regularly deploys the Sichuan based 149 Motorised Division in the TAR, as it did in the wake of the Tibetan demonstrations in Lhasa in 1987 and thereafter. China is also planning to shift the headquarters of the TAR Military District from Chengdu to a site located to the southwest of Lhasa, along the road to Gongkar airport. The new complex, under construction, includes about 40 three-storey buildings, each containing about 40 rooms, and capable of accommodating up to 15,000 men.

Xinjiang and Qinghai under Lanzhou Military Region has the 61st Rapid Reaction Division stationed at Tianshui and the 12 Armored Division, stationed at Zhangye in Gansu province. The 4th Motorised Infantry Division of Xinjiang Military Region is located quite close to the Afghanistan border. The 6th Motorized Infantry Division, stationed at Kashi, is the only mechanized combat unit in the Xinjiang Military Region. It is also close to Afghanistan and is located right in the heart of southern Xinjiang. Should Uighur independence activities break out of control, the above two divisions would be the first to be dispatched. Urumqi, the capital of Xinjiang, it is under the 11th Brigade. 26th Group Army is stationed in the Xinjiang Military Sub Region. The 63 Armed Police Division and 7 Infantry Division are under the 21st Group Army and are stationed at the cities of Pingliang and Ili, respectively. The largest military bases in Tibet under Lanzhou Military Region are at Silling, Chabcha, and Karmu. All the three places also have air force bases. Golmud is also a major military base. Located strategically to cover both Tibet and Eastern Turkestan, this region is connected by road, rail and air. The Chinese military build-up in Kham and Ngapa regions are concentrated in Lithang, Kanze, Tawu, Dartsedo, etc. in Kham sub-district, and Barkham in Ngapa sub-district. However, there are radar stations and dormant air strips in Kham sub-district at various localities.

China also has a listening post in Aksai Chin. Sources say the listening stations will monitor Indian deployments in the region, eavesdrop on forward and intelligence communications of the army and even intercept US radio signals pertaining to anti-terrorism activities in Afghanistan.

Six Chinese Air bases are located in Chengdu Military region. These are Chengdu, Chongqing, Kumming, Lhasa, Mengzi and Xinning. Six others located in Lanzhou Military region could also be used against India. These are Urumqi, Wugong, Wulumqi, Yanliang, Yinchuan, Kashi (Ref: website globalsecurity.org)

Mobilization

China could move one rapid reaction division, the 149th from the Chengdu Military Region and one rapid reaction division, the 61st Plateau Rapid Reaction Motorised Division of No. 26 Group Army under the Lanzhou Military Region to Tibet to meet any emergency within days. Some additional airborne troops, rapid reaction troops and armed police could be directly delivered to Lhasa from the air. The No. 15 Airborne Division could be air-dropped to Tibet and equipment such as airborne fighting vehicles could be put to use. China will need to induct another six to eight divisions for launching any major offensive. That could take at least a month.

Nuclear Weapons

China has nuclear installations and testing facilities in Northern Tibet. The first nuclear weapon was brought onto the Tibetan plateau in 1971 and stationed in the Tsai dam basin, in the north-eastern district of Amdo. As China's ground-based nuclear missiles can be transported and fired from trailers, efforts to locate and count missiles in certain areas remain difficult.

China's primary nuclear weapon research and design facility, known as the "Ninth Academy" is located in Haiyan in Amdo District. It was responsible for designing all of China's nuclear bombs through the mid-seventies. It also served as a research centre for detonator development, radiochemistry and many other nuclear weapons related activities. China is believed to have nuclear manufacturing centers at Haiyan and Huangyuan in Amdo.

Missiles

The Chinese have deployed a large number of missiles in Tibet. Most of these are targeted at Indian cities. It is reported that there are eight missile bases containing at least eight ICBMs, seventy MRBMs, twenty IRBMs and 17 Radar Stations in TAR. The missile bases are located to the south of Lake Kokonor in Amdo and Nagchukha. China has established a nuclear missile deployment and launch site for DF-4 missiles (China's first inter-continental ballistic missile) in the Tsai Dam basin at Haiyan. Another nuclear missile site in Tibet is located at Delingha, about 200 km south-east of Larger Tsai Dam. It also houses DF-4s and is the missile regimental headquarters for Amdo. A new nuclear division has also been established in Amdo. Four CSS-4 missiles are reported to be based there, which have a range of 8000 miles, capable of striking the United States, Europe and all of Asia.

Conclusion

In spite of the improved infrastructure, the Chinese Army will have certain operational problems in Tibet. These are listed below:

- Long axes of maintenance which can be disrupted by weather, Tibetan resistance and enemy action.
- Requirement of acclimatization of troops and adverse effects of high altitude on men, animals and material.
- A sullen local population not reconciled to Chinese occupation.
- Reduced airlift capability due to high altitude conditions.

Grant of asylum to Dalai Lama and his followers after his flight to India in 1959 is seen as a hostile act by China. China feels that the Khampa rebellion of 1959 was aided and abetted by India in collusion with Western powers. Establishment of Tibetan government in exile in India has only aggravated matters. Efforts by the Dalai Lama to keep alive the issue of Tibetan independence/autonomy and seek world support further angered the Chinese. China follows a policy of zero tolerance to disruptive activities in TAR and Xinjiang. It therefore maintains adequate troops in the region.

Tibet, irrespective of China's tight control remains volatile. Although the Dalai Lama has relinquished his demand for total independence, his continued stay in India and the large support he enjoys in the Western World will keep the pot boiling. How this issue is finally resolved will have a major bearing on Sino-India relations. The Tibetan youth are getting restless and are convinced that the non-violent movement is being seen as Tibetan weakness and would not lead to any tangible results. Tibetan youth may well adopt the Indian model of seeking independence from British rule through the combination of non-violent and violent movements. So long as China perceives that India is supporting the Tibetan movement, it will always be suspicious of Indian motives and an uneasy peace will continue to prevail between these neighbors. If unrest spreads in Tibet, China may adopt the option of going to war with India and try to settle the problem once for all.

It will also be seen that the main Group Armies of Chengdu Military Region which is responsible for operations in TAR, the 54th, 13th and 14th are not located in TAR but in Sichuan and Yunnan Provinces in peace time. This is primarily for administrative and logistic convenience. Troops within TAR are mainly of holding and defensive nature. Any major offensive through Tibet will require induction of additional troops from Lanzhou and other Military Regions possibly Beijing or Jinan Military Regions which are connected by rail to Tibet. However, there are many logistic bases in Tibet which holds requirements of ammunitions, rations, fuel, equipment and spares that may be required for a war.

India's Military Problems

10

The Indian Army

The army has a strength of about 1.2 million. As per the website www.globalsecurity.org, it is divided into five regional commands, Eastern, Western, Northern, Southern and South Western. It has 12 corps with 3 armored divisions, 4 RAPID light mechanized divisions, 18 infantry divisions, 10 mountain divisions, two artillery divisions, five independent armored brigades, five independent infantry brigades, three independent artillery brigades, four air defence brigades, and three engineer brigades.

The Eastern Command is responsible for operations in Sikkim, Bhutan, Line of Actual Control with China in Arunachal and borders with Burma (Myanmar) and Bangladesh. It has three Corps. III Corps is located at Dimapur. It has two divisions, 57 Mtn Div at Leimakong (Manipur) and 23 Infantry Division at Ranchi. It appears to be responsible for borders with Myanmar and Bangladesh. IV Corps is located at Tezpur. It has three divisions. 2 Mtn Div at Dibrugarh, 5 Mtn Div at Bomdila and 21 Mtn Div at Rangia. A fourth division may be under raising here. The Corps is responsible for defence of Arunachal's borders with China. The Corps is also engaged in counter insurgency operation in Assam. XXXIII Corps is located at Siliguri. It has three divisions. 17 Mtn Div is at Gangtok, 27 Mtn Div is at Kalimpong and 20 Mtn Div is at Binnaguri. It is responsible for defending Sikkim, Bhutan and the Siliguri Corridor.

The Northern Command is responsible for operations in Jammu & Kashmir and Ladakh, both against China and Pakistan. It has got three Corps. XIV Corps is located at Leh. It has two divisions, 3 Mtn Div at Leh and 8 Mtn Div at Dras. XV Corps is located at Srinagar. It has two divisions, 28 Mtn Division at Gurais and 19 Inf Div at Baramula. XVI Corps is located at Jammu. It has two divisions,10 Inf Div at Akhnoor and 25 Inf Div at Rajauri.

Western Command is primarily responsible for operations against Pakistan. It is also responsible for India's borders with China (Tibet) that lies between Ladakh and Nepal. It has one strike corps, the II Corps and two holding corps, IX Corps and XI Corps. II Corps is located at Chandigarh and has 1 Armd Div and 40 Arty Div at Ambala, 14 RAPID at Dehradun and 22 Inf Div at Meerut. IX Corp has three divisions, 26 Inf Div at Jammu, 29 Inf Div at Pathankot and 39 Inf Div at Yol. XI Corps is located at Jalandhar. It has three divisions, 15 Inf Div at Amritsar, 7 Inf Div at Ferozepur and 9 Mtn Div at Meerut.

South Western Command is responsible for operations against Pakistan. It has one strike corps, I Corps and one holding Corps, X Corps. I Corps has 33 Armd Div at Hissar, 4 Inf Div at Allahabad and 6 Mtn Div at Bareilly. X Corps has 16 Inf Div at Ganganagar, 18 RAPID at Kota and 24 RAPID at Bikaner.

Southern Command is responsible for operations against Pakistan and defence of Andaman & Nicobar Islands. It has one strike corps, the XXI Corps and one holding Corps, the XII Corps. XXI Corps has 31 Armd Div at Jhansi, 36 RAPID at Sagar, 54 Inf Div at Secunderabad and 41 Arty Div at Pune. XII Corps has two holding divisions, 12 Inf Div at Jodhpur and 11 Inf Div at Ahmedabad.

Indian Air Force

India's Air Force, the world's fourth largest, has over 600 combat aircraft and more than 500 transport planes and helicopters. The air force is deployed into five operational commands, the Western Air Command, headquartered at New Delhi, the South-western Air Command, headquartered at

Jodhpur, the Eastern Air Command, headquartered at Shillong, the Central Air Command, headquartered at Allahabad and the Southern Air Command, headquartered at Thiruvananthapuram (Trivandrum), Kerala. The airforce consists of about forty squadrons. Each squadron has about 16 to 20 aircraft. Its combat fleet has Sukhoi 30s, Mirage 2000, Jaguars, MiG 29s, MiG 27s and about 230 MiG 21s (To be phased out). It has about 200 transport planes including Boeings, IL-76, An 32, BAe-748 etc. It has attack helicopters, heavy transport helicopters, medium transport helicopters and light helicopters. It has about 280 surface to air missiles, (SAM). (Source: www.globalsecurity.org)

Overall Comparison Between the Armed Forces of India, Pakistan and China

Item	India	Pakistan	China	Remarks
GDP in Billion US $ (2008)	1209	167	4401	
Foreign Exchange Reserves Billion US $	265	12	2131	As of June 2009
Defence Budget 2007-08 in Billion US $	30	5.2*	70	*Pakistan gets an undisclosed amount of military aid from the US ostensibly to fight terror but is used to strengthen its army against India.
Army				
Total Manpower in million	1.2	0.8	1.6	
Military Commands/ Regions	5	5	7	
Corps / Group Armies	12	8	18	
Armored Divisions	3	2	7	
Mechanised Divisions	4*	4	3	* RAPIDS
Motorised Divisions	0	0	24	

Item	India	Pakistan	China	Remarks
Infantry / Mountain Divisions	28	15	15	
Amphibious Assault Division	0	0	2	
Artillery Divisions	2	1	9	
Independent Armored Brigades	5	?	12	
Independent Infantry/ motorised Brigades	5	?	24	
Independent Artillery Brigades	3	?	14	
Total Tanks	5000	2450	7580	
Air Force				
Total Personnel	1,70,000	65,000	2,50,000	
Total Aircraft	1330	530	2300	
Air Bases	61	9	>150*	Six each in Lanzhou and Chengdu Military Regions
Combat Aircraft	780	390	1,500	
Navy				
Total Personnel	?	?	2,90,000	
Aircraft Carriers	1	0	0	
Destroyers	8	0	26	
Frigates	13	7	49	
Corvettees	24	5	14	
Nuclear Submarines	0*	0	8	* One on lease from Russia
Submarines	16	8	55	
Nuclear warheads	70-100	30-40	100-400	

The Verdict

Simple comparison of overall military strengths as given above does not give an actionable or understandable picture regarding relative military strengths of countries. India deploys troops against China and Pakistan. Pakistan deploys troops against India as also in Baluchistan and on Afghan border. China deploys forces against Afghanistan, Mongolia, Russia, North Korea, Taiwan, Vietnam, Laos, Myanmar and India. What is important is to be able to estimate what one country can deploy against another in time of war. This has been attempted later in this chapter. It is not out of place to mention that Pakistan and India are almost evenly matched head to head in nuclear and missile capabilities. China has a definite edge over India.

Indian Navy is larger in fleet strength and with a more varied range of ships including an aircraft carrier while Pakistan's Navy is smaller and has no aircraft carrier. However, Pakistan has a very small coastline and economic zone to defend and its requirement of naval forces is limited. Chinese navy is substantially superior to the Indian Navy particularly in its submarine strength. But the Indian coastline is very far from the nearest major Chinese naval base at Hanian Island. Till China acquires fully functional naval facilities in Myanmar, Bangladesh, Sri Lanka and Pakistan and stations ships and submarines there on a permanent basis, its capability to act against the Indian Navy will remain limited.

In the area of conventional ground forces, both the Indian as well as Pakistani Army is well-equipped and highly trained to survive in extremes of topography and climate. The Chinese Army has a definite edge over India in conventional forces.

The real source of military power is economic power. Here China is way ahead of India and India is way ahead of Pakistan. If each country spends an equal percentage of GDP on defence, the disparity will continue to grow. Pakistan's foreign exchange reserves are precarious. However, rich Muslim countries like Saudi Arabia and Libya could come to its aid in case of war with India.

Comparison with Pakistan

This book is not about the threat to India from Pakistan. China has not militarily assisted Pakistan in the Indo-Pak wars of 1965 and 1971. Neither did it militarily support Pakistan in its misadventure at Kargil in 1999. However, that does not mean that China and Pakistan cannot come together during any future conflict. China and Pakistan are close allies. They share military equipment, animosity towards India and a desire to cut India to size. Both have substantial border disputes with India. They can come together during any future war. India's defense thinking and concerns have mostly been Pakistan oriented. It is therefore interesting to know where we stand vis-à-vis Pakistan, China and their combined forces in Kashmir.

Pakistan Army

The Pakistan Army is divided into five military regions, Punjab, Sindh, J&K, FANA, NWFP & FATA and Baluchistan. (Refer Map: 7). It has a total of eight corps consisting of two armored divisions, four mechanized divisions, fifteen infantry divisions and two artillery division. The order of battle of Pakistan Army as obtained from the website www.globalsecurity.com is given below:

Punjab Military Region. This region is responsible for Pakistan's border with Punjab, Haryana and the northern part of Rajasthan. It holds all Pakistan's offensive forces which consist of I Corps and II Corps. I Corp located at Mangla is composed of 6 Armd Div (Kharian), 17 Mech Div (Kharian) and 37 Mech Div (Gurjanwala). II Corps located at Multan is composed of 1 Armd Div (Multan), 14 Inf Div (Okhra) and 40 Inf Div (Okhra). The military region has three holding corps or defensive corps as given below. A holding corps is supposed to be capable of launching limited offensives, spoiling attacks or diversionary attacks.

- IV Corp located at Lahore is composed of 10 Inf Div and 11 Inf Div, both located at Lahore.
- XXX Corps located at Gujranwala with 8 Inf Div and 15 Inf Div both located at Sialkot.

- XXXI Corps located at Bhawalpur with 25 Mech Div and 35 Inf Div both located at Bhawalpur. Some believe that 40 Inf Div at Okhra, shown under II Corps is actually a part of this Corps.

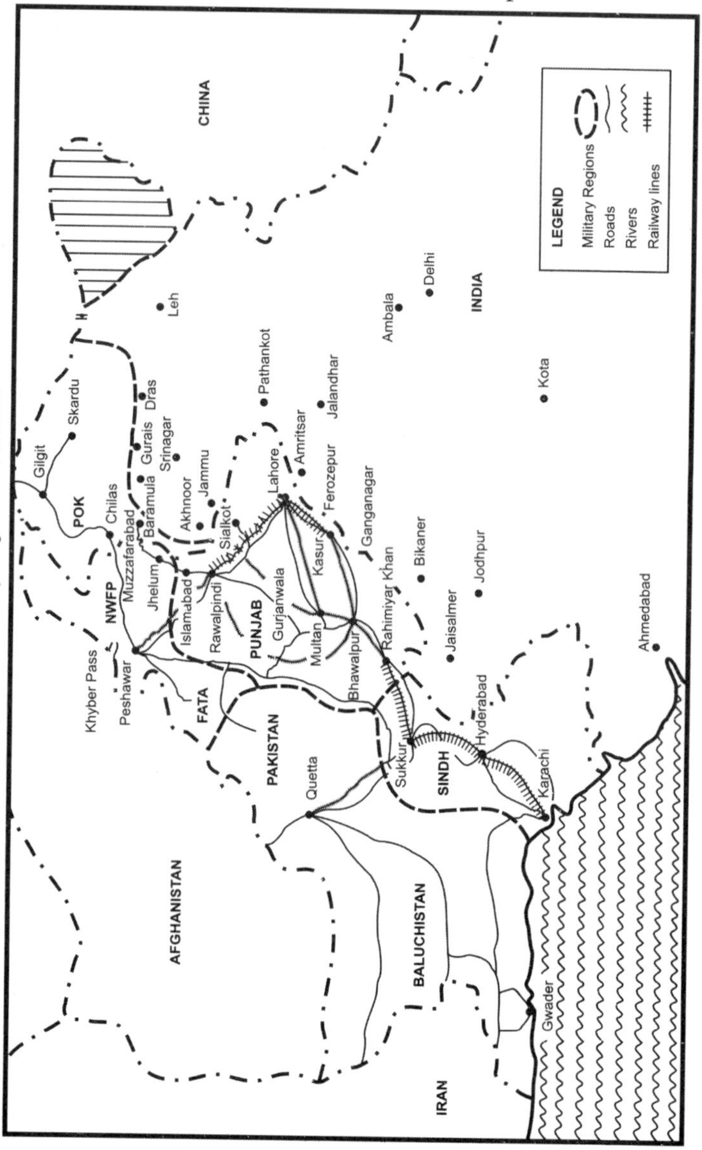

Map No. 7: Military Regions of Pakistan

Sindh Military Region. This region is responsible for Pakistan's borders with southern Rajasthan and Gujarat. It has only one corps the V Corps located at Karachi in the region. V Corps is composed of 16 Inf Div and 18 Inf Div at Hyderabad and 35 Mech Div at Malir.

J&K and FANA Military Region. This military region is responsible for Pakistan's Line of Control in Jammu and Kashmir and Ladakh. There is only one corps in the region, X Corps located at Rawalpindi. The corps consists of Northern Area Command (POK), 12 Inf Div (Muree), 19 Inf Div (Jhelum/Rawalkot) and 23 Inf Div at Mangla.

NWFP/FATA Military Region. This military region is responsible for Pakistan's borders with eastern Afghanistan. It is also supposed to be fighting Taliban and Al Qaeda. The region has one Corps the XI Corps located at Peshawar. It has 7 Inf Div located at Mardan and 9 Inf Div at Kohat. One division could be withdrawn and sent to the east in case of a war with India.

Baluchistan Military Region. This military region is responsible for Pakistan's borders with southern Afghanistan and Iran. Pakistan is fighting a separatist insurgency in the region. The region has only one Corps, the XII Corps located at Quetta. It has two infantry divisions, 33 Inf Div and 41 Inf Div at Hyderabad (Sindh). One division could be withdrawn and sent to the east in case of a war with India.

Comparison of Indian and Pakistani Holding Formations (See Map: 8)

India		Pakistan		Remarks
Corps/Div	Location	Corps/Div	Location	
XIV Corps*	Leh	X Corps	Rawalpindi	*3 Mtn Div of this corps is facing China
8 Mtn Div	Dras	Northern Area Command*	POK	*The troops are locals formed into Northern Light Infantry. Strength over one division

(*Contd...*)

India		Pakistan		Remarks
Corps/Div	Location	Corps/Div	Location	
XV Corps	Srinagar	12 Inf Div	Muree*	*alternately at Muzaffarabad in POK
19 Inf Div	Baramula	19 Inf Div	Jhelum*	*alternately at Rawalkot
28 Inf Div	Gurez	23 Inf Div	Mangla	
XVI Corps	Jammu	XXX Corps	Gujranwala	
10 Inf Div	Akhnoor	8 Inf Div	Sialkot	
25 Inf Div	Rajauri	15 Inf Div	Sialkot	
IX Corps	Pathankot	IV Corps	Lahore	
26 Inf Div	Jammu	10 Inf Div	Lahore	
29 Inf Div	Pathankot	11 Inf Div	Lahore	
39 Inf Div	Yol	XXXI Corps	Bhawalpur	
XI Corps	Jallandhar	26 Mech Div	Bhawalpur	
15 Inf Div	Amritsar	35 Inf Div	Bhawalpur*	*or at Gujranwala
7 Inf Div	Ferozpur	40 Inf Div	Okhra	
9 Inf Div	Meerut	V Corps	Karachi	
X Corps	Abhor	25 Mech Div	Malir*	*or at Karachi
16 Inf Div	Ganganagar	16 Inf Div	Hyderabad*	*or Rahimiyar Khan
18 RAPID	Kota	18 Inf Div	Hyderabad	
24 RAPID	Bikaner			
XII Corps	Jodhpur			
12 Inf Div	Jodhpur			
11 Inf Div	Ahmedabad			
Seven corps, two RAPIDS and fourteen divisions		Five corps, two mech divs and twelve inf divs		India thus has two divisions more than Pakistan on its western border. A small difference.

Map No. 8: Comparison of Holding Formations

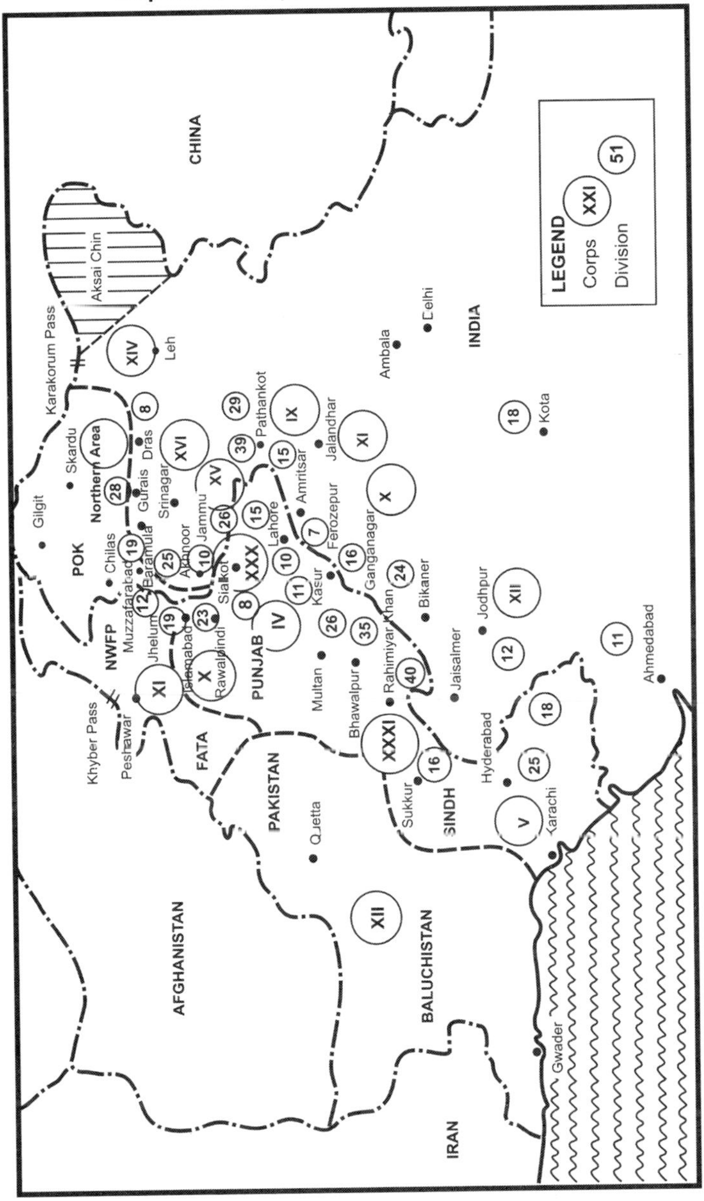

Offensive Formations

India		Pakistan		Remarks
Corps /Div	Location	Corps/Div	Location	
II Corps	Chandigarh	I Corps	Mangla	
1 Armd Div	Ambala	6 Armd Div	Kharian	
14 RAPID	Dehradun	37 Mech Div	Gujranwala*	*or Sukkur
22 Inf Div	Meerut	17 Mech Div	Kharian	
40 Arty Div	Ambala	2 Arty Div	Gujranwala	
I Corps	Mathura	II Corps	Multan	
33 Armd Div	Hissar	1 Armd Div	Multan	
4 Inf Div	Allahabad	14 Inf Div	Okhra	
6 Mtn Div	Bareilly	12 Arty Div	Multan	
XXI Corps	Bhopal			
31Armd Div	Jhansi			
36 RAPID	Sagar			
54 Inf Div	Secunderabad			
41 Arty Div	Pune			
Three Corps consisting of three armd divs, two RAPIDS, four inf/mtn divs and two arty divs.		Two corps consisting of two armd divs, two mech divs, one inf div and two arty divs.		India has an additional offensive capability of one corps HQ, one armd div and three inf divs. This can be diverted to meet a Chinese threat if required.

It will be seen from above that India enjoys a slight superiority in both holding and offensive formations. It has an advantage of two divisions in holding formations. This advantage can be neutralized by Pakistan by shifting two divisions from Afghan border and Baluchistan. India has an advantage of one armored division and three infantry divisions in offensive forces. The advantage over Pakistan is not overwhelming. The border between the two countries in Punjab and the lower reaches of Kashmir have well prepared permanent defences, anti-tank ditches and defence oriented canals and are defended in strength. It is unlikely that either side can make any major breakthrough in these sectors. Neither side could penetrate more than 15 to 20 km during 1965 and 1971 wars. Those who keep advocating that India should attack Pakistan if it continues to support terrorism need to study the above figures and be acquainted with the reality. Pakistan is well aware of its limitations in a conventional war with India. That is why Late President Zia ul Haq initiated his strategy of "Bleeding India from a Thousand Cuts" through Pakistan sponsored terrorism in Kashmir and north-eastern India. If India wants a decisive military superiority against Pakistan, it should raise one more offensive corps of one armd div, one RAPID and two inf divisions. Economic constraints will make it difficult for Pakistan to match such an increase and sustain the additional defence expenditure over a long period.

Pakistan Air Force

The Pakistan Air Force has a strength of about 65,000. Its headquarters is in Rawalpindi. The air force is organized into eighteen (fifteen according to some sources) squadrons, with a total of about 335 combat aircraft. The number is expected to increase to 390 by 2015. Its interceptors or air defence aircraft includes Chinese J-6s (which are to be replaced by J-10s) and J-7s. In ground-attack role they have Chinese Q-5s (being replaced by JF-17), Mirage IIIs and Mirage Vs, one squadron of which is equipped with Exocet anti-ship missiles and deployed in an anti-ship role. Pakistan also has about 60 F-16s. The latest acquisition into the Pakistani Air Force is the JF-17 aircraft from China. The assembly of JF-17 aircrafts in Pakistan has commenced and eight to ten aircrafts will be assembled per year. Pakistan is also reported to be acquiring up to eight Erieye airborne surveillance system mounted on Saab 2000 aircraft of Sweden. Pakistan is reported to have placed an order for the Chinese AWACS system ZDK-03 based on Chinese Y-8 aircraft. Pakistan has purchased 50 Mirage IIIs and Vs, 150 sealed pack engines and a huge quantity of Mirage spares from Libya. The Mirage Rebuild Factory, which is a part of PAC, had been rebuilding the 35 year old version of the Mirage aircraft which were bought as scrap from various countries. The PAF is acquiring 2 Squadrons of the Italian Falco UAV. Eventually, the PAF plans to field 5-6 UAV Squadrons. The backbone of the transport fleet is twelve C-130 Hercules. To enable Pakistan to fight Taliban and Al Qaeda, the United States has delivered some refurbished C-130E transports, refurbished P-3C surveillance aircraft, refurbished Cobra helicopters, new Bell 412 helicopters and a number of Harpoon missiles, AN/TPS-77 surveillance radars, night vision goggles and AIM-9M Sidewinder missiles. The equipment will be used against India if required. Pakistan has also purchased some MI-171 helicopters from Ukraine for its Special Services Group (SSG). Pakistan has purchased four CN-235 air craft from Indonesia for VIP travel.

India has a slight edge over Pakistan in air force capability. Indian pilots are also reputed to be better trained and more capable in air combat than Pakistani forces. But neither country can achieve complete control of the air and both air forces can cause considerable damage to the other, the ground forces and civilian infrastructure during wars.

Comparison with China

The details of the Chinese Army have been given in Chapter 3 and the deployment of Chinese Army in Tibet has been covered in Chapter 9. The comparison of Indian and Chinese forces is given on the next page. (Ref Map: 9)

Comparison of Indian and Chinese Holding Formations along LAC & Arunachal Border

India		China		Remarks
Corps/Div	Location	Corps/Div	Location	
III Corps	Dimapur	Yunnan Military District	Myanmar Border	
57 Mtn Div	Leimakong	Armed Police Div	Myanmar Border	Armed Police Divisions were formed in 1983 when the border security responsibility was transferred to Ministry of Public Security. 14 Chinese army divisions (500,000 men) were transferred to Armed Police in 1990 when the Army's strength was reduced by 500,000.
IV Corps	Tezpur	Sichuan Military District	Sichuan Province	
2 Mtn Div	Dibrugarh	Armed Police Div	*	*Opposite Tezu-Walong sector of Arunachal Pradesh
5 Mtn Div	Bomdila	Xijang Military District	*	*Entire Tibet Autonomous Region (TAR)
21 Mtn Div	Rangia	41 Armed Police Div	?	Possibly located south and east of Lhasa opposite Sikkim and Tawang
XXXIII Corps	Siliguri	38 Armed Police Div	?	Possibly located in Western Tibet

(Contd...)

India		China		Remarks
Corps/Div	Location	Corps/Div	Location	
17 Mtn Div	Gangtok	149 Rapid Reaction Div*	Leshan, Sichuan Dist	*Immediate Reserve for entire TAR
27 Mtn Div	Kalimpong	Other Troops*	TAR	*These consist of 52 and 53 Independent Mechanized brigades, over six Armed Police Regiments, artillery and other support units
20 Mtn Div	Binnaguri	Xinjiang Military Dist	Xinjiang* Province	*Including Aksai Chin
XIV Corps	Leh	63 Armed Police Div	Pingliang	
3 Mtn Div	Leh	6 Mot Inf Div	Kashi	
New Mtn Div	*	61 Rapid Reaction Div	Tianshui	*Being raised somewhere
I Corps	Mathura	7 Inf Div	Ili	
6 Mtn Div	Bareilly			
A total of nine to ten mtn divs, one on Myanmar Border, three for Arunachal, three for Sikkim and Bhutan, one for Himachal Pradesh and Uttarakhand and one for Ladakh		A total of about six regular divisions and six armed police divisions. One armed police div on Myanmar border, two opposite Arunachal, one in western TAR and one in Xinjiang. Two regular divs in TAR and three in Xinjiang.		The two sides are almost at par in holding forces.

Offensive Capability

India		China		Remarks
Corps /Div	Location	Corps/Div	Location	
		13th Group Army*	Myanmar Border	*In addition to the two divisions, it has an independent armd bde, atry bde & an AAA bde
		Mot Inf Div	Myanmar Border	
		Inf Div	Myanmar Border	
		14th Group Army*	Kumming	*In addition to the two divs, the group has an independent armd bde, AAA bde, engr regt and pontoon regt.
		Inf Div	Kumming	
		Arty Div	Kumming	
		54 Group Army*	Xincheng	*In addition to the two divs, the group has an independent armd bde, a mech inf bde, an arty bde, an AAA bde and an engr regt. It operated in Tawang sector in 1962 Indo-China war.
		Mot inf div	?	Location not known
		Light mot inf div	?	Location not known
		Xinjiang* Military Dist	Xinjiang dist	The troops mentioned are in addition to the holding formations and can be used along with some

(Contd...)

India		China		Remarks
Corps /Div	Location	Corps/Div	Location	
				holding troops for a offensive against Ladakh
		Armd div	Xinjiang dist	
		Mot inf div	Xinjiang dist	
India has no offensive capability against China. Neither does it have any counter attack capability.		Two group armies with three inf divisions, two armd bdes and supporting units in the east, one group army with two divisions and support troops against Tawang or Siliguri and one army group with two to three divisions against Ladakh		The offensive forces can be further increased by induction of other group armies and another five to six divisions from other military regions. India, on the other hand, will find it hard to pull out troops from Pakistan border.

It will be seen that though India has parity in holding troops vis-à-vis China, it has absolutely no forces which can match China's offensive capability along the "Old Burma Road" in Walong, Lehkapani sector. India is reasonably equipped to defend Tawang-Bomdilla axis. China can attempt to bypass the strong Indian defenses in Sikkim by trying to reach Siliguri through western Bhutan and cut-off the lines of communications to Assam and the north-eastern states. India does not seem to have any reserves in the Eastern Command to react to any unexpected thrusts in the east.

Missile Capabilities of China and Pakistan

Introduction

China's strategic missile forces have been discussed in brief in Chapter 3. China is miles ahead of India's nuclear forces in nuclear defence and delivery systems. China, has started stockpiling its nuclear arsenal in 1964. It has 200 to 400 nuclear warheads. The most powerful ones among China's nuclear arsenal have yields of over 4 megatons. In comparison, India's strategic nuclear stockpiling started after the 1998 nuclear tests. It is reported to have about 50 to 70 warheads at present. The most powerful among India's nuclear warheads has an yield of 0.05 megatons which is minuscule, compared to China. Agni 2, India's longest range, deployed ballistic missile is capable of a range of 2500 km. It can carry a single nuclear warhead of 1000 kg. In contrast, China's nuclear delivery system is far more advanced than India's, with multi-warhead MIRV capable ICBMs like DF-5A and DF-4. It also possesses submarine launched ballistic missiles (SLBMs) like JL-1 which has a range of 4500 km. China also has bomber aircrafts like IL76 (range 1800 km), Tu16 (range 4500 km) and ground attack aircraft like Q-5 (range 500 km) and J-11/Su-27 (range 1800 km) which can deliver nuclear warheads.

Pakistan's ballistic missile effort is largely India centric. The US supplied F-16 combat aircraft are capable of delivering nuclear warheads. But, perhaps due to periodic US sanctions which affect the combat readiness of the F 16 fleet and Indian air defence capabilities, Pakistan has opted to rely more on land based ballistic missile systems as the mainstay of Pakistan's nuclear strike force. Pakistan's missile projects are managed by the National Defence Complex (NDC), a subsidiary of the Pakistan Atomic Energy Commission (PAEC) which was formed in 1993. The Khan Research Laboratories (KRL) is also an important part of Pakistan's missile development program. In the early 1990s, the NDC acquired complete though unassembled M-11s and possibly an undisclosed number of M-9 Short Range Ballistic Missiles (SRBMs) from Beijing. During the mid-1990s, China apparently transferred an entire production line for M-11s and possibly M-9s to the NDC.

Pakistan has relied extensively on North Korea for its liquid propelled ballistic missile program. North Korea is alleged to have supplied Pakistan with 12-25 operational Nodong ballistic missiles and their launch vehicles. North Korean assistance has also included technical support, including missile launch and telemetry crews. Analysts speculate that North Korea may have also transferred an entire production line of the Nodong ballistic missiles to KRL. Pakistan will remain dependent on North Korea for importing complete liquid engines or at least their major component parts, as well as the liquid propellants to fuel its missiles for some more years. Some statements attributed to Pakistani nuclear scientists and government leaders suggest that the Ghauri-II will have a range of 1,700 km; other statements suggest that the Ghauri-III will have a strike-range of 2,000-3,500 km. The Ghauri-II and III may be North Korean Taepodong missiles. Pakistan test fired Ghauri II missile in 1999. Islamabad also plans to develop the Babur missile for deployment on aircraft (such as F-16, Mirage-5) and submarines (Agosta 90B). Operational missiles are inducted into the Army Strategic Forces Command.

Details of Pakistani and Chinese Missiles

Pakistani Name	Chinese Name	Payload kg	Range km	Remarks
Hatf I, IA		500	60-100	Single stage, solid motor, non nuclear, probably obsolete
Hatf II or Abdali		500	290-300	2 stage solid motor trailer mounted
Hatf III or Gaznavi	DF-11 or M-11	500-800	250 -300	Single warhead, trailer mounted, solid propellant ballistic missile. Pakistan has imported 30 to 80 from China and deployed at Sargodha air base.
Hatf IV or Shaheen I	DF-15 or M-9	500-800	750-800	Single warhead, road mobile, solid propellant SRBM with 300m circular error probability (CEP)
Hatf V or Ghauri I	-	1000	1200-1300	Liquid propelled, road mobile MRBM said to be the North Korean Nodong missile. Pakistan reportedly imported 12 to 25 Missiles in 2003.
Not with Pakistan	DF 2 & 2 A	1300	1250	Solid fuel road mobile introduced in Chinese army in 2003.
Hatf VI or Shaheen II	DF 21 or M-18	400-500	1800-2000	Two stage, solid fuel, road mobile MRBM in service with Pakistan since 2007

Pakistani Name	Chinese Name	Payload kg	Range km	Remarks
Hatf VII or Babur	DH-10	?	1500-2000	A sub-sonic cruise missile developed by China from an unexploded US Tomahawk cruise missile found by Pakistan in Afghanistan and passed to China.
Hatf VIII or Ra'ad		?	350	Air launched cruise missile under development in Pakistan. Supposed to have stealth capabilities.
Not with Pakistan	DF 3A	3000		Solid fuel MRBM in service in China since 1971
Not with Pakistan	DF 4	4500-5000		Multi warhead MIRV capable MRBM
Not with Pakistan	DF 5	12000-13000		Multi warhead MIRV capable ICBM
Not with Pakistan	DF 31	8000		An improved version of DF 4 introduced in 2003
Not with Pakistan	DF 41	12000		An improved version of DF 5 possibly still under development.

Analysis

India is in the process of acquiring either the Israeli Arrow-2 or the U.S. PAC-3 missile defence systems. This could spur significant changes in Pakistan's missile programs. Pakistan's ground based cruise missile programs seems aimed to nullify the Indian ballistic missile defences. An Indian theater missile defence would not create a fool proof defence umbrella. But a limited missile defence coupled with improvements in Indian long-range air and satellite-based reconnaissance capabilities could reduce the deterrence value of a Pakistani SRBM force. In such a scenario, Pakistan is likely to seek Chinese help to develop intermediate range ballistic missile systems, land and sea launched cruise and ballistic missiles which could defeat India's missile defences.

It will be clear from above that Pakistan and China have a potent arsenal of nuclear capable ballistic missiles with a maximum range of 1800 to 2000 km in case of Pakistan and 8000 km in case of China. Both have ground and air launched cruise missiles with a range of up to 700 km. China has submarine launched cruise and IRBMs. Hence Delhi, Mumbai and most Indian cities are within range of Pakistani and Chinese missiles.

My concerns regarding Pakistan's and China's nuclear and missile capability are:

- Are our civil and military command and control centers, ammunition depots and other strategic targets adequately camouflaged and hardened to absorb a nuclear strike and continue to operate?
- Is the chain of command of our government and armed forces laid down as is done in the US to ensure that there are no breakdown of the command structure in case of a nuclear strike on our capital?
- Do we have any contingency plans to restore communication with in an operationally acceptable time frame in case a major bridge on the Jammu-Pathankot highway or in the Eastern Command is destroyed by enemy missiles or air?

Threat Perceptions

I have no access to the threat perceptions from Pakistan and China based on which the Indian Government, Ministry of Defence and the Armed Forces Headquarters have arrived at our force levels, deployments and modernization programs. However, the past performance of the Indian Government in this regard is not exactly inspiring.

India was totally unprepared for Pakistan's attempt to annexe Kashmir by force in 1947. Srinagar could be successfully defended only, because the Pakistani attackers spent two days in raping and plundering Baramula. (May I suggest that the readers of this book also read a book called "Outstanding Victories of the Indian Army" written by me and published by Lancer Publishers and Distributors, New Delhi for details of some of the battles referred to in these paragraphs). And, after more than a year of hard fought battles and thousands of casualties, just when the Indian Army had started making good progress in pushing Pakistanis out of Kashmir, the Indian Government declared ceasefire and enabled Pakistan to hold on to the northern and western part of Kashmir, an area known today as Pakistani Occupied Kashmir (POK). I am not privy to whether the ceasefire was declared because of external pressure or because Pandit Nehru wanted to be known was a world statesman rather than a nationalist leader. In any case the damage has been done.

The Indian Government did not learn any lessons from the Pakistani attack on Kashmir. Pandit Nehru and Mr. Krishna Menon, his worthy defence minister, firmly believed that India and China were brothers and China would never attack India. So confident were the two in this belief that no effort was made to modernize and strengthen the defence forces to make it capable of defending India. Krishna Menon ordered ordnance factories to produce coffee percolators instead of weapons and ammunition. Few know that he was so unhappy with the frank views of Lt. Col. Sam Manekshaw (who led the Indian army to victory in the Bangladesh war in 1971 and was made Field Marshal) that he had Manekshaw posted as the commanding officer of a girl's NCC battalion. Fortunately for India, Krishna Menon was sacked after the Chinese debacle and Manekshaw's brilliant military career was revived.

Indo-Chinese relations began to deteriorate in 1959 when Dalai Lama and his followers were granted asylum in India. This made the Government of India mildly apprehensive. The Border Roads Organization was established in 1960 to develop roads in border areas. Some ill equipped troops were inducted into the border areas of Ladakh and NEFA without adequate winter clothing. Ladies were asked to weave sweaters, socks and gloves for the soldiers. Families were asked to gift gold ornaments to the Government's National Defence Fund so that it could buy weapons. Lieutenant General B.M. Kaul, a Kashmiri Pandit (Nehru's clan) with no combat experience was made the General Officer Commanding IV Corps. But it was too little, too late. When the Chinese attacked in October

1962, there was utter chaos. The general officer reported sick and fled to Delhi. In less than a month, the Chinese Army had swept all resistance, taken Bomdila and reached the foothills in Assam. Nehru, in a broadcast to the nation on 18 Nov 1962, admitted that India was not in a position to defend Assam and bid the people of the North-east goodbye. Just when the stunned people of Assam were trying to figure out what to do, the Chinese announced ceasefire and withdrew.

In 1958, Pakistan under General Ayub Khan allied with the US and NATO and joined the SEATO and CENTO military treaties. Thereafter, it started receiving latest US tanks, armored personnel carriers, artillery and aircraft. It is inconceivable that the Indian Government was not aware of the developments. The government choose to ignore the military build-up in Pakistan. No effort was made to upgrade Indian tanks and artillery. The only modernisation was that the bolt action .303 rifles were replaced with 7.62mm Self Loading Rifles (SLR). India survived the Pakistani attacks in 1965, without any serious territorial losses and without any upgradation of their military hardware, only because of the Chinese attack of 1962. After the Chinese attack, all army units were made full strength in officers and men. There was great emphasis on training. There was a full complement of junior officers ready to lead from the front. India was also helped by some inept Pakistani generalship which failed to exploit their superiority in armored forces in the battle of Khemkaran.

Lal Bahadur Shastri became the Prime Minister after Nehru. He was a nationalist. His slogan "Jai Jawan, Jai Kissan", laid the priorities of the nation as defence preparedness and growth in agriculture. He led India during the Indo-Pak war of 1965. Under his leadership, the Indian army not only successfully defended all Pakistani attacks, an attempted takeover of Kashmir by air drop of Pakistani special forces into the Kashmir valley but captured the Pakistani territory known as the Haji Pir Bulge. Shastriji did not complete his term. He died mysteriously while negotiating the ceasefire terms at Taskent. India meekly agreed to return Haji Pir to Pakistan.

Indira Gandhi succeeded Shastri as India's Prime Minister. She was a true nationalist and arguably the best Prime Minister India has had to date. She believed that India needed to be militarily strong. She concluded a peace and friendship treaty with the Soviet Union and modernised the Indian Army. Tanks, artillery, armed personnel carriers, aircrafts, helicopters and ships were imported from Russia. The soldiers and officers were fully trained and motivated. So India had the upper hand in the Indo-Pak war of 1971. Bangladesh was liberated in spite of US use attempt to intervene with its Seventh Fleet to save its ally.

Indira Gandhi was succeeded by Prime Ministers who were more pacifists and economists than nationalists. The old belief, "there will be no war and if there is war, I will not be in the chair to fight it" was back. Defence budget was slashed at the behest of IMF. The eighteen years of peace that followed pushed defence requirements for modernisation into the background. Normalisation of relations with Pakistan, the so-called people to people contact, introduction of bus and train services were going on and being hailed in the media. India chose to downplay Late Pakistani President Zia ul Haq's strategy of "Bleeding India from a Thousand Cuts"(fostering terrorist activities in Kashmir and other parts of India). It reacted defensively, accepting casualties of security personnel and innocent civilians and increasing security for political leaders. This was sharply different from Shastriji's instruction to the army to go for terrorist bases in POK. So the inevitable happened. Pakistani infiltrators quietly occupied the Indian posts on the LOC in Kargil Sector in 1999. India claims to have won the war that followed and having evicted the infiltrators. But Pt. 5353 remains in Pakistani hands and Pakistan flaunts it as its victory in the Kargil war. It leaves me wondering as to what is our threat perception against Pakistan and what is our desired military capability vis-à-vis Pakistan.

Another question which agitates my mind is what is our threat perception vis-à-vis China? George Fernandes is the only political leader who said that China is India's number one enemy. He has also denied having ever said the same. However, from the time of Sun Tzu (500 BC), it is recognized that the only pragmatic and prudent approach to threat perception and defence preparedness is to go by capabilities and not by intentions of possible adversaries. Intentions can change with a change of government or a head of state. And God knows that in today's violent and volatile world, it does not take much time to change governments or intentions. But it takes a long time to build a deterant military capability. Pakistan may have aggressive intentions but it does not have a decisive edge in military capabilities. China may not have any apparent aggressive intentions. But it certainly has a substantial edge in military capabilities. It is also imprudent to ignore the growing military capabilities of Bangladesh, however insignificant it may appear. Alone, it may pose a minor military threat to India. But in association with China, it can play a decisive role in any war against India, particularly at the Siliguri Corridor. Our learned threat perception specialists may also like to remember an old adage, "Hope for the best and prepare for the worst".

Threat Perception to Kashmir

Before we examine the threat to Kashmir, it may be appropriate to briefly recapitulate the various battles which have been fought in this sector. (Ref MAP: 9) The first attack on Kashmir was by Pakistan in 1947. The attacks were over the entire border but concentrated on four main thrust lines as under:

- *Northern Thrust*: Gilgit-Skardu-Gurez/Kargil/Leh. The Northern Thrust was through what is known as the Northern Areas of POK and lies mostly along the Indus Valley. The attackers met stiff resistance at Skardu Fort which, though isolated, held out for almost a year till they ran out of ammunition. All men were killed and all women were raped. But their heroic resistance saved Ladakh. The attackers were able to occupy Gurais, Zozilla Pass and Kargil almost unopposed and laid seize to Leh. The Indian Army recaptured Gurez, Zojilla, Kargil and relieved Leh in 1948.
- *The Central Thrust*: Jhelum-Muzaffarabad-Uri-Baramula-Srinagar. This thrust was along the main

road from Pakistan to Srinagar. The Kashmir State Forces and the Indian Army somehow managed to defend Srinagar and later pushed the attackers back to Muzzafarabad.

- *Poonch Sector*: The Pakistani attack on Poonch was repulsed. However, the territory between Uri and Poonch, known as the Haji Pir Bulge remains in Pakistani hands.
- *Rajauri Sector*: Here, the Pakistanis were initially able to capture Rajauri. However, the Indian Army was able to recapture it in 1948.

The second attack on Kashmir was by the Chinese in 1962. China already controlled most of the disputed territory of Aksai Chin. India held a few posts in Shyok Sector called the Chip Chap Valley, Galwan Valley and Dulat Beg Oldi. It had also built an airfield at Chusul near the Indian Border with Tibet near the Pangong Lake. The Chinese launched two thrusts against these positions on 20th October, 1962.

- *The Shyok Sector*: The Chinese attacked from Aksai Chin through the Pamzal River Valley. The Indian outposts and garrisons in the Sector were over run by the superior Chinese troops in a few days.
- *Chusul Sector*: The Chinese attacked from Tibet south of Pangong Pso. Chinese captured Gurung Hill by 20th October and attacked Rezangla in strength on 22nd October. The Indian Army somehow managed to hold on to the air field till the ceasefire on 21 November.

The third attack on Kashmir was during the Indo-Pak Wars of 1965. Pakistan attempted to capture Kashmir in August 1965 by infiltrating and air dropping Special Forces. However, the Pakistanis did not get the local support they expected and the operation failed. The Indian Prime Minister, Lal Bahadur Shastri then ordered the Indian Army to launch attacks at militant bases in POK. Indian troops launched the attacks on 15 August, 1965 and captured Haji Pir. Pakistan gained some ground in Tithwal, Uri and Poonch sectors. On September 1, 1965, Pakistan launched a major attack to capture Akhnoor near Jammu to cut-off the main supply routes to Indian troops in Kashmir. The attack made initial gains but was unable to capture Akhnoor.

Map No. 9: J&K Sector

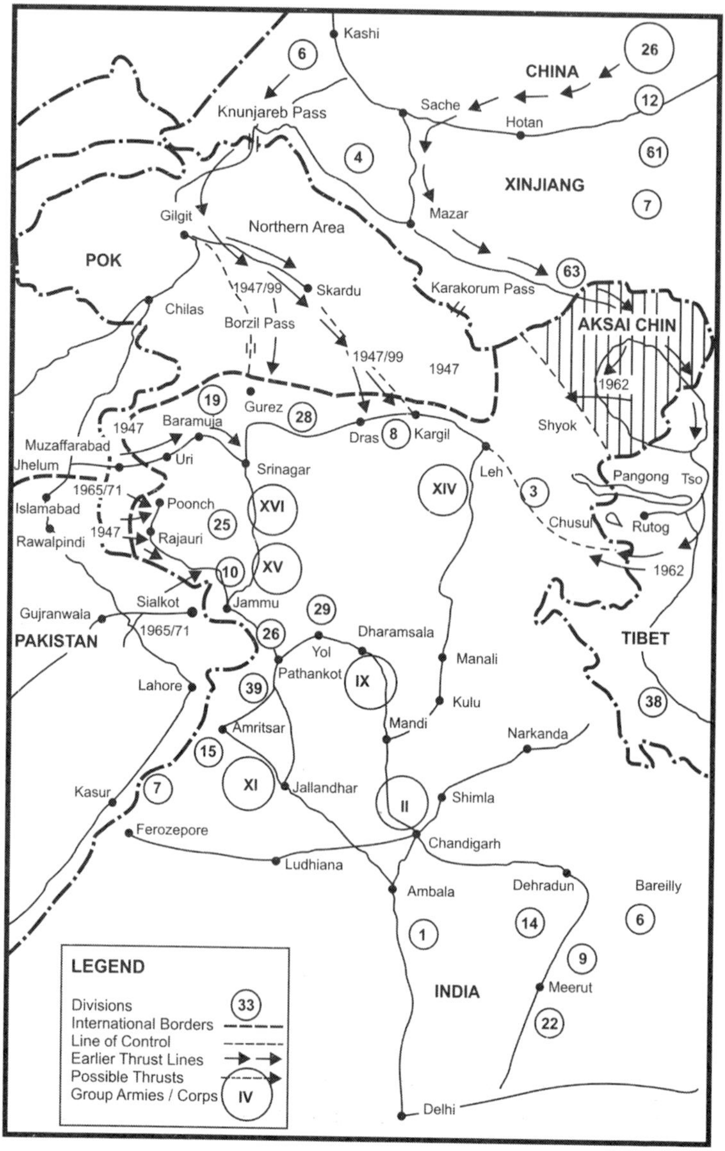

The fourth attack on Kashmir was during the Indo-Pak war of 1971. There were two main Pakistani thrusts in the Kashmir sector. These are described below. The Indian Army then made a series of small attacks and captured several Pakistani posts north and west of Poonch. Indians secured all Pakistani outposts which overlooked the Zoji La Pass and Kargil.

- *Poonch Sector*. Pakistani 26 Inf Bde attacked Poonch on 3rd December but were repulsed.
- *Jammu Sector*. Pakistan's main offensive was launched by its II Corps in Chhamb sector north of Jammu on December 3. Here, the Pakistani 23 Inf Div overwhelmed the forward defensive positions of the Indian 10 Inf Div. Two days later, the Pakistanis took the town of Chhamb and established a bridgehead on the east side of the Munawar Tawi river. On December 10, the Indians counter-attacked, sending the Pakistanis back across the river. In the next two days, units of Pakistani II Corps recrossed the river twice only to be forced to withdraw. By December 12, the sector stabilized.

The fifth attack on Kashmir was in May 1999, when Pakistani special forces managed to infiltrate and occupied most of the heights which dominate the Srinagar-Leh road in the Kargil Sector. It took more than a month of bitter hand to hand fighting by the Indian Army to recapture most of the heights. One height, Pt. 5353, still remains in Pakistani hands.

It will be seen from above that Pakistan has made four attempts to capture Kashmir or parts of Kashmir by force. Each time the Indian Army has successfully thwarted the attempts. It is unlikely that Pakistan can ever succeed unless it attacks Kashmir in association with China. When China attacked Ladakh in 1962, it was not trying to capture Ladakh. It was only establishing its authority over areas which it claimed as its own. But things have changed. China's military power is far greater than what it was in 1962. It has more than six divisions in the Xinjiang Province adjoining Aksai Chin and another two to three divisions in the Lanzhou military region. A major portion of these forces can take part in any offensive against India in Kashmir and Ladakh. The Karakorum

Highway connecting Xinjiang and Gilgit enables a part of the Chinese forces to attack Kargil or Leh through POK.

Another threat which is often underestimated is the threat from various insurgent groups operating in the area. They are quite capable of disrupting lines of communications by destroying bridges and attacking logistic convoys with roadside bombs and ambushes.

My main concerns are:

- Does our threat perception for Kashmir takes into consideration the possibility of Pakistan and China joining hands in an attempt to annexe Kashmir which is a disputed territory? Are we prepared to face and defeat a forces of six to seven divisions against Ladakh?
- Does the threat perception include the threat to lines of communication from insurgent groups operating in the area and provide for their protection and restoration?
- Do we have a military capability to deal with terrorist training camps in POK with pin point strikes or by any other method?

Threat Perception Eastern Command (Refer: Map No. 10)

Before we talk about threat assessment to our Eastern Command, it will be relevant to examine what happened during 1962 and the Bangladesh war and the geopolitical changes that have taken place in the region since 1962. Chinese troops launched attacks in the Eastern Sector on 20 October, 1962 along three thrust lines as described below:

- **Tawang Sector**. This was the main thrust. China attacked the southern banks of the Namka Chu River on 20 October. The Chinese easily routed the ill-equipped, foolishly deployed (the Indian Army's 7 Inf Bde was holding the bridges of a fordable Namka Chu instead of the heights of Tsangdhar) by bypassing them and attacking them from the rear. On 23rd October, the Chinese launched a three pronged attack on Tawang and captured it. There followed a lull of about three weeks while China improved tracks and built-up its forces. The Chinese then cut-off Se La by capturing Thembang and attacked Se La and

Bomdila on 17 November. They again routed the Indian forces without a fight. By 18 November, the Chinese had reached within 17 km of Tezpur.

Map No. 10: Eastern Sector

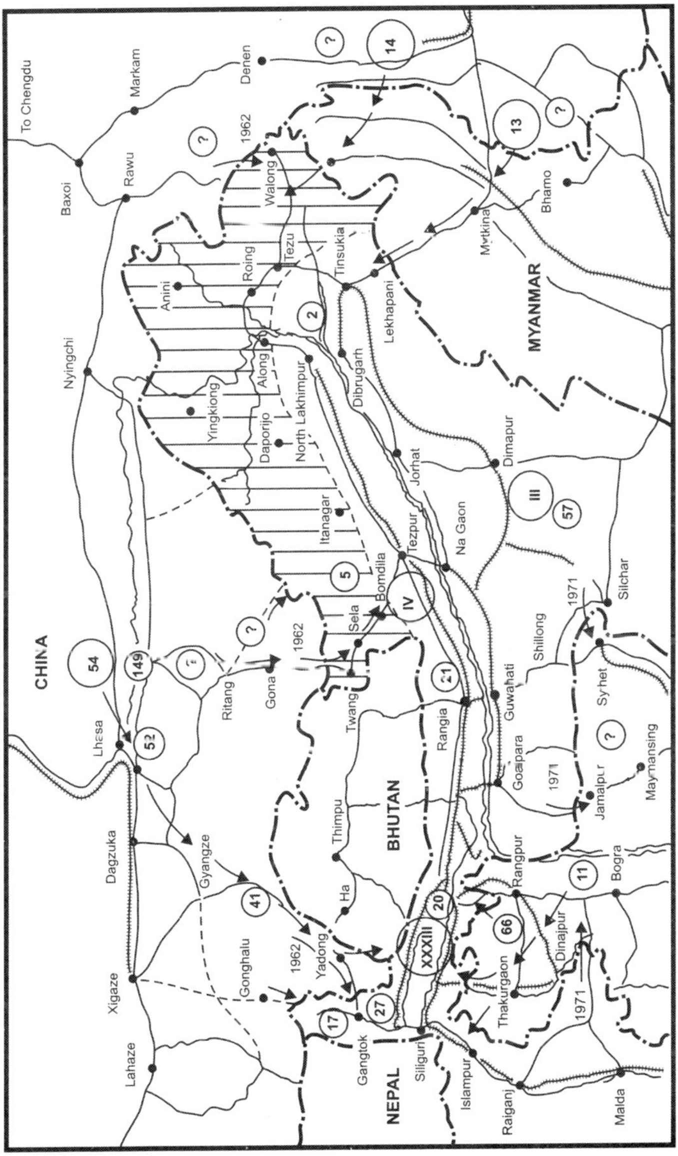

- **Walong Sector.** This was a subsidiary thrust. Chinese shelled Walong defence on 22 October and attacked it on 23rd October. Walong was captured by the Chinese with heavy casualties on both sides. There followed a lull of about three weeks. The Indian Army attempted to recapture Walong on 14 November, but failed. The Chinese did not attempt to move deeper into Indian territory.
- **Siliguri Sector.** There were only skirmishes in this sector at Nathu La on Sikkim-Tibet Border. China managed to secure most of the disputed territory without serious fighting.

The Indian government was in the process of evacuating the territories north of the Brahmaputra river on 18th November. On 21st November, China unilaterally declared ceasefire and withdrew to positions it held prior to 20 October, 1962 and thus saved the Indian government of a major embarrassment. There were two reasons for the reprieve. India had applied to the West for help on 3rd November. The United States informed India that it could not provide military assistance to India unless India agreed to negotiate with Pakistan on the Kashmir dispute. Nehru agreed to negotiations. In return, U.S. then provided India a $60 million emergency military aid. The second reason was that the passes on the Tawang axis were going to be snowbound during winter and maintaining a large force south of the watershed would have been difficult.

During 1971 War of Liberation, the Indian Army launched five main thrusts into then East Pakistan. The bases for these thrusts were Agartala, Silchar, Meghalaya, North Bengal, Raiganj and Kolkata. These thrust lines are marked on the Map: 9. If Bangladesh allies with China in any future conflict, it could use any of the thrust lines to attack India and tie down Indian forces which could be deployed against the Chinese. It could also attack and cut-off the narrow Siliguri Corridor and trap the Indian XXXIII and IV Corps.

Another threat which is often underestimated is the threat from various insurgent groups operating in the area. They are quite capable of disrupting lines of communications by destroying bridges and attacking logistic convoys with roadside bombs and ambushes.

Some of the geopolitical changes that have taken place since 1962 which are relevant to threat assessment are listed below:

- Chinese military and logistic capabilities are far superior today than what it was in 1962. The network of roads on both sides of the border are far better and can sustain large forces. The Xinning-Lhasa railway enables China to build-up forces in Tibet much faster than ever before.
- Myanmar was hostile to China in 1962. Hence China could not use north Myanmar and the Old Burma (Ledo) Road of World War II for its attack on Walong sector. However, the ruling military junta of Myanmar has been totally dependent on China for military, economic and political support since 1988. China also has two group armies or corps on Myanmar-China Border and Kumming. So, China can easily attack India through northern Myanmar along the Old Burma Road in any future conflict.
- In 1962, there was no Bangladesh and Pakistan did not have a military alliance with China. Bangladesh joined the Chinese bandwagon in 1976. Bangladesh today has seven well-trained divisions equipped with Chinese and Pakistani arms. Is their any guarantee that Bangladesh will not side with China in any future conflict and seek North Bengal, Assam and some of the other north-eastern States as its share of the booty? Insurgents and liberation movements of all these states are based in Bangladesh.

My concerns regarding the treat assessment in Eastern Command are:

- Does the threat perception take into account the capability of the Chinese Army to launch anything up to four to six divisions through northern Myanmar and along the Old Burma Road in Walong-Lekhapani Sector? The terrain in this sector is far more conducive to operations by large forces all year around than the Tawang Sector and is poorly defended.

- Does the threat perception take into consideration the possibility of Bangladesh joining hands with China in any future conflict and trying to cut-off the narrow Siliguri Corridor?
- Does the threat perception take into account the changing geopolitical environment described above?
- Does the threat perception include the threat to lines of communication from insurgent groups operating in the area and provide for their protection and restoration?

Cyber Warfare Capability

China has repeatedly demonstrated its cyber warfare capability by hacking into US networks in Pentagon and even the White House. Modern day warfare uses computers and electronic communication in every operating system, communication system and for command and control. Electronic and cyber warfare thus assumes great importance.

My concern is:

- Have we developed adequate defensive cyber warfare capability to prevent enemy attacks on our systems and prevent the enemy from accessing sensitive data and attack our systems?
- Do we have offensive cyber warfare capability which can access enemy data and disrupt enemy operating systems?
- Cyber warfare requires exceptionally talented, computer savvy, eccentric individuals who are incapable of being selected into the armed forces. Do we have real talent working in the field or are we trying to make do with officers and men who are "Jack of all trades" on a rotational assignment and tenure system?

Intelligence Gathering Capability

India has been repeatedly plagued by intelligence failures. Indian Government was unaware of Chinese road building activities in Aksai Chin till the road had been completed. In 1971, India had very little topographical information about Bangladesh. In 1974, when I was serving in a brigade which was trying to stop a gang of Naga Militants returning after training in China, the SIB never provided any actionable intelligence. All information about Naga militant camps were of those that had been abandoned. Every one knew where the SIB office was. When someone wanted money or rum, they would go to the SIB, tell them a story and collect what they wanted. We do not seem to have any underground organization for collecting intelligence. In 1999, we had no information that Pakistan had infiltrated the Indian Posts and was occupying heights on the LOC in the Kargil Sector. Could we not have carried out an aerial reconnaissance before sending Capt. Saurav Kalia and his patrol to their death? Is the Army Aviation Corps helicopters which replaced the Air Observation fixed wing aircraft only meant for VIP travel. Successful military operations cannot be planned unless we have accurate informations about the terrain and enemy strengths and activities. Intelligence is required for acquiring targets to be neutralized by artillery, air or missiles and a host of other information. India has satellite based intelligence systems, radio monitoring units and other electronic listening systems. There are Google maps which can give excellent terrain information. There are many websites like globalsecurity.org, nti.org, which maintain an updated orbat and other information about all armies of the world.

My concern is:

- Whether our military and other intelligence systems are properly organized and staffed with dedicated and competent staff to gather intelligence about terrain and enemy activities on a real time basis and provide actionable intelligence to our government and the armed forces?

- Do the Chief of Staffs of the various services, the defence minister and the national security advisor visit the various intelligence set ups and see for themselves whether they are adequately staffed with motivated and competent staff and are functioning satisfactorily?
- Are our intelligence systems headed by a professional intelligence cadre or by IAS, IPS or General Staff cadre army officers who are on a rotational tenure assignment and only trying to get a good ACR and get a promotion?

Conclusion

China seems to have a grand strategic design in South Asia, basically focused on the strategic encirclement of India. The unfortunate reality for India is that it has no friends in South Asia. India needs to break out of the strategic encirclement imposed by China by providing large scale military and economic aid to Vietnam. China and Vietnam are enemies who have fought each other and have border disputes and disputes over economic zones on their coast. We can conclude a treaty of friendship and cooperation with Vietnam on lines of what China has with Bangladesh. It may cost a few billion dollars but we have the foreign exchange reserves to afford it.

India also needs to lessen the conventional and nuclear weapons gap with China. India's ICBM and SLBM development programs need to be strengthened. It will do well to raise a number of additional infantry and mechanized divisions to protect its vulnerable communication bottle necks, the Siliguri Corridor which extends from Siliguri to Jogigopa and its border with Myanmar.

It is obvious that China is pursuing its strategic interests to have a clear access to the Indian Ocean by providing military and economic aid to Myanmar and Bangladesh. The triangular relationship of these three countries, China-Pakistan-Myanmar, should be of concern to India. The insurgency problem in the North-eastern states of India cannot be controlled effectively without the help from Myanmar and Bangladesh. Despite India's efforts in improving its relations with Myanmar with its proactive "Look East" policy, Pakistan and China can influence Myanmar to foment trouble at any time. Myanmar has officially confirmed in January 2002, that it is building a nuclear reactor with aid from Pakistan and China. It is also likely that these countries are already having an intelligence sharing agreement regarding India's force deployment in the North-East and the Bay of Bengal. This is crucial especially in a war or war-like situation.

India must also acquire an offensive capability of a Corps Headquarters and at least three divisions under Eastern Command which can be used to prevent Chinese annexation of Myanmar and to counter attack and regain any territorial losses in the sector.

Part 3
Other Reasons for Concern

Economic Reasons for Concern

11

China's Economic Power

China is arguably the world's number one economic power. It may not have the largest investment capital, the highest GDP or per capita income in the world. But it has the world's highest foreign exchange reserve of about $2.2 trillion which is more than twice that of Japan, four times that of EU, five times that of Russia and about eight times that of India. This huge foreign exchange reserve enables China to access technology and natural resources all over the world and buy political influence in our neighbouring countries through economic and military aid. China is also the largest holder of US Treasury bonds and US debt. It can destabilize the dollar whenever it chooses to by simply redeeming the US Treasury Bonds or selling a few billion US dollars on the world's foreign exchange markets. China has been demanding that the US dollar should be replaced by an SDR as the world's trading currency. China has prevented the Asian Development Bank from providing a loan to India for development of Arunachal Pradesh.

I am concerned that:

- Our neighbours like Pakistan, Bangladesh, Myanmar, Sri Lanka and Nepal will become totally dependent on China's military and economic aid for survival and in turn will be compliant to Chinese instructions to act against India, whenever and in whatever manner China wants them to act.

- China may arm twist Pakistan, Bangladesh, Myanmar and Nepal to align with it in any future conflict with India.
- China will put economic pressure on the US to deny Indian technologies and to remain neutral in any military conflict.
- India is investing large sums of its meagre foreign exchange reserves in US Treasury Bonds in an environment where both the US economy and the US dollar is precariously poised at the mercy of China and may collapse any day.

India's Trade Deficit vis-à-vis China

The Chinese ambassador Sun Yuxi had predicted in May 2007 that China will surpass US as India's largest trading partner. He expected the bilateral trade to surpass the target of $40 billion before 2008 and reach $80 billion by 2010. India and China gave a major push to their ties by signing 11 agreements in 2008 covering issues ranging from economic planning to housing, health and culture. The two sides also agreed to triple bilateral trade target to $60 billion against the previous target of $40 billion within four years. Bilateral trade figures are misleading. It does not indicate which side is exporting more and is therefore the gainer. For example, the US had a trade deficit of about 750 billion US dollars more than half of which is in bilateral trade with China. Cheap Chinese imports have completely destroyed US and European manufacturing. Cheap Chinese imports if allowed unchecked will destroy Indian manufacturing. Since we can export almost nothing to China except ores and slag, our trade deficit will keep on growing till a situation will come when our economic and foreign policies will be dictated by China. Let us see the figures below:

Summary of India-China Trade

Year	2001	2002	2003	2004	2005	2006	2007	2008
Trade volume in Billion US $	3.6	4.9	7.6	13.6	18.7	25	38.7	51.78
India's balance of trade Billion US $	–0.2	–0.4	–0.81	+1.78	–3.0	–4.0	–9.6	–12.0

China imports only raw materials like ores, slag and organic chemicals from India which is beneficial for Chinese industries and generate employment in China. On the other hand, India imports finished goods like steel, machinery, mobile hand sets, electric bulbs, toys and a host of other product to the detriment of Indian industry and loss of jobs in India. Mr. Vajpayee's government earned a China friendly image by steadfastly refusing to heed the protectionist pleas of Indian industry that raised the bogey of Chinese goods swamping Indian markets. China has been pushing for an FTA with India for sometime, but this is forcefully opposed by Indian businesses and companies who fear Indian markets being flooded by cheap imports from China. India's trade deficit with China is becoming politically sensitive for the government.

I am concerned that:

- Cheap imports from China will destroy Indian industry in the same way as it has destroyed US manufacturing and create large scale unemployment. This will destroy the Indian economy in the same way as it has destroyed the US economy.
- Our government will continue to pander to vested interests of importers and middlemen and refuse to protect the Indian industry, the Indian economy and the Indian nation.

Poor State of India's Defence Production

India spends billions of dollars on procurement of military hardware. It is sad that unlike China, Myanmar or Pakistan, even after sixty years of independence, we do not produce even 10 per cent of our defence requirements. Indigenous production of defence equipment not only guarantees availability of it during war but also generates employment and increases GDP. India can produce rockets which launch satellites, ships and nuclear submarines. Why can it not produce tanks, artillery pieces, helicopters and fighter aircraft? Why is the Defence Research and Development Organization (DRDO) unable to develop the equipment we require and produce the same. One reason which I am aware of is the Qualitative Requirement (QR) of the equipment which is drawn up by the service headquarters. The simple way of doing it is to take out Jane's Weapons of the World and list the best of each performance parameter of the equipment available with each country and produce the QR. It is like my saying that my daughter-in-law should have the looks of Aishwaria Rai, physical fitness of Saina Nehwal, personality of Kiran Bedi and compassion of Mother Teresa. It is obvious that I will never find a daughter-in-law and DRDO will never be able to develop such an equipment. There is a complete lack of pragmatism. If Mahindras had not started with the licensed production of the World War II version of the Willy's Jeep, it would not have been able to design and produce state of art SUVs like the Bolero or the Xylo. Our generals and bureaucrats do not encourage indigenous development of military equipment. So we have to depend on imports for all we need and all those associated with the deal, politicians, bureaucrats and generals, will enjoy the cutbacks. The other likely reason is that Indians love foreign made things and our leaders and generals are so used to foreign brands that they cannot be satisfied with any thing made in India.

My concern is that:

- Because of vested interests, in spite of having a world class industrial base, we will continue to import military hardware which can easily be produced within the country and make defence production beneficial for the economy of the country.
- For the same reasons and pressure from unions, we will not allow participation of private sector industrial houses into defence production.
- With the signing of free trade agreement with ASEAN, cheap Chinese products will get re-exported to India and increase our trade deficit.

Conclusion

Economic power is the source of military power. Economic power is not increased by importing all kinds of consumer goods and military hardware and having a large trade deficit. Even the US is reluctantly trying to learn the simple reason for the collapse of the American economy. Can any Indian, political leader, bureaucrat general, businessman or sportsman overcome the lure of foreign brands and be satisfied with Indian brands and Indian products? Can our military produce pragmatic qualitative requirements and encourage indigenous production of defence equipment by reputed industrial houses within the country? If we cannot, we will perish.

Political Reasons for Concern

12

Degradation of the Armed Forces since Independence

India is a only country in South Asia, where the armed forces have been banished from the ruling elite of the country. They have absolutely no say in the policies of the government. Their requirements are forgotten during times of peace. Take the issue of the MiG 21s which have claimed the lives of more pilots than any war. The courts of the country do not allow vehicles which are more than 15 years old on the roads of Indian metros. But they do not bar warplanes which are more than thirty years old from being in the inventory of the armed forces. And our leaders expect them to out perform Chinese J-10 or J-17s. The armed forces are only remembered when there is a crisis like Kargil or when the insurgency situation in some part of the country goes out of hand. The situation is completely different in Pakistan, Bangladesh, Myanmar and China. Pakistan has been ruled by the army for almost half the years since independence. Even when not ruling the country, the Pakistani Armed Forces have veto powers over foreign policy of the civil government. The defence requirements of funds have the topmost priority in government expenditure. Pakistani government has no powers to sack the Chief of Army Staff or the Head of ISI. USA and Britain openly acknowledge that elements in the Pakistan Army and ISI are supporting militants, particularly when they are engaged in furthering the strategy of making India "Bleed from a thousand cuts". China has never been ruled by the armed forces. But the autocratic regime of China firmly believes that "Political Power Comes from the Barrel of the Gun" and top generals have always been close to their policy making authority. The needs of the armed forces have the top most priority. Will the IAS allow the generals to have decision-making authority in matters of defence?

Weak Decision-Making Ability

Indian democracy is weak in decision-making. Governments have not had a clear majority since 1990 and are more pre-occupied in saving the government and their power and perks than saving the country. In a democracy, the interests of individuals in power come first, the interests of the party come second and the interests of the country come last always and every time. In such an environment, defence requirements do not have any priority. To the best of my knowledge, there have been only two defence ministers who took interest in the armed forces. One was Arun Singh, the minister of state for defence under Rajeev Gandhi, who resigned over the Bofors deal and the other was George Fernandes who visited Siachin more times than many army chiefs and dared ask the bureaucrats of Ministry of Defence to visit Siachin and get to know the problems of the defence forces first hand. Decisions on acquisition of military equipment are unpopular and politically risky as any purchase will be questioned in the parliament and allegations of kickbacks will cloud all deals. How can urgently required equipment be acquired in time under such an atmosphere?

Timid Leaders

Most Indian Prime Ministers have been timid pacifists. Nehru's policies with regard to defence preparedness led to the debacle of 1962. The credit for India having a well equipped and trained army goes to Mrs. Indira Gandhi who modernized the armed forces and led India to victory over Pakistan in 1971. Narsimha Rao regime cut defence budget and stopped modernization of the armed forces. Vajpayee showed some guts in carrying out the nuclear tests, restarting modernization of the armed forces and solving the married accommodation problems of the armed forces. He also took on Pakistan over Kargil. But his "OP PARAKRAM" where the Indian Army remained deployed on the borders for a year in response to the terrorist attack on the Indian Parliament was a pathetic display of indecision. And now we have Prime Minister Manmohan Singh telling the parliament that whatever be the provocation, "War is not an option". Indira Gandhi could defy the US and liberate Bangladesh. Vajpayee could defy the US and carry out nuclear tests. But Manmohan Singh seems incapable of resisting US pressure to talk to Pakistan without preconditions and to sign defence deals with end use agreements which dilute the sovereignty of our nation and prevent the acquired equipment being used against Pakistan.

My concern is:

- The Indian government's attitude of peace at all cost is going to encourage Pakistan and China to seek unacceptable concessions in Kashmir and Arunachal. It will also encourage China to seek a solution to the boundary issue by force.
- India's inability to resist pressure to sign end-use agreement for weapons acquired from US will make it impossible for us to use these arsenal against Pakistan.
- We will never acquire the capability to attack and defeat Pakistan in face of provocations or acquire the military capability to give a bloody nose to China should it seek to militarily impose its will on us.

Swinging Towards the US

American self interests and whims have always dominated US foreign policy. It has a history of abandoning its non-European allies if it felt that a country or a regime was not following its dictates or going against American interests. The acceptance of the Hyde Act which includes many do's and don't clauses like India must support US efforts to prevent Iran from producing nuclear weapons and halt increase in nuclear weapons arsenal in South Asia (meaning India) illustrates the malaise. Let us see some examples of American betrayal of its allies:

- **Cuba.** The U.S. had liberated Cuba from Spanish rule and de-facto ruled the country thereon to 1959. Castro had started the Cuban revolution in 1956. The U.S. had been firmly on the side of President Batista who had been elected for the second time in 1955. The U.S. had inducted a Military Advisory Group to assist President Batista and was providing military and financial aid to the right wing, anti-communist, pro-U.S., Batista regime in its fight against the revolutionaries. Then suddenly in March 1958, the American regime under President Eisenhower stopped military supplies to the Batista Regime and imposed trade sanctions over human rights abuses. They even persuaded Batista to step down on January 1, 1959, allowed Fidel Castro to takeover power and recognized his government on January 7, 1959.
- **Pakistan.** Pakistan joined the U.S. and NATO alliance in 1958 by joining SEATO and CENTO treaties. It received military and economic aid which encouraged it to attack India. But just because it had not obtained U.S. permission for doing so, the US stopped military supplies including spares during the war. It again stopped supply of F-16 aircraft which had been paid for to Pakistan when it carried out nuclear tests in 1998. Pakistan has stopped relying on the US for military supplies and banks on China for weapons and military supplies.
- **Lebanon.** U.S. and its NATO allies have always supported the Christian elements of Lebanon and opposed pro-Syria, pro-Palestine elements. The UN Security Council passed Resolution 425 calling for an immediate Israeli withdrawal and creating the UN Interim Force in Lebanon. This force was given the responsibility of maintaining peace after Israeli forces withdrew which really meant ensuring that Muslims did not get an upper hand. The international force was composed of U.S. Marines, French and Italian units. Two truck bombings struck the U.S. embassy

and U.S. marine barracks. Unable to accept the casualties, the Americans withdrew and left Lebanon under Syrian influence. They had also abandoned South Vietnam and Cambodia allowing Vietnam to be unified under the communist regime and Cambodia coming under Vietnamese domination.

- **Georgia.** Ever since the collapse of the Soviet Union in 1991, the U.S. has been trying to wean away the countries which broke away from the Soviet Union and bring them under U.S. and NATO influence. Georgia is one of these countries. The US encouraged the Rose revolution and rejoiced when President Saakashvili assumed power in 2004. Military and economic aid flowed in and Gerogia became a part of President Bush's "Coalition of the willing" and sent troops to Iraq. In 2008, President Saakashvili, confident of U.S. support, attacked the breakaway regions of Abkhazia and South Ossetia. When the Russians counter-attacked and almost took over Georgia, the U.S. did very little. It certainly did not intervene militarily.
- **Khampa Rebellion.** The U.S. supported the Khampa Rebellion in Tibet with funds and weapons through CIA. Most of the aid was channeled through Nepal. But suddenly, in 1969, during Kissinger's overtures to China, they abandoned the Khampas in favour of relations with China.

These were a few examples of U.S. reliability as an ally. There are many others like Iraq, and Somalia. There are many examples of American arrogance like justifying a body search of Ex-President A.P.J. Abdul Kalam amongst a host of other lesser Indians. We meekly tolerate such nonsense and refuse to retaliate. Today, the Indian Government is enthusiastically proclaiming "US-India Bhai Bhai". I hope our learned and honourable political leaders are aware of the U.S. track record as an ally before ditching the Soviet Union and hitching their future to the self-seeking American Administrations.

I am concerned that:

- Our government is gullible and getting taken in by American sales talk. The G-8 resolution that India must sign the NPT and the pressure on our Prime Minister to talk to Pakistan are clear indicator of things to come.
- The end user agreement for sale of American weapons to India is being taken too lightly. Only a few are aware that India did not attack East Pakistan in 1965, because the Indian divisions in the Eastern Command were equipped with American small arms and winter clothing and their end user agreement did not permit India to use them against Pakistan.

Chinese Support to Insurgents in the north-east

China provided financial and military support to Naga insurgents in the seventies. At least three Naga insurgent groups, each more than a hundred strong had gone to Yunnan province of China through north Myanmar to receive military training and equipment. Though there have not been reports of similar support to insurgents in recent times, there were some reports that ULFA was trying to shift its base from Bangladesh to Yunnan Province of China.

My concern is that:

- China will also adopt the Pakistani strategy of "Bleeding India from a thousand cuts" by aiding the various insurgent groups operating in the north-east either directly or through its allies like Bangladesh and Myanmar before launching an attempt to annexe Arunachal Pradesh by force.
- Our timid government will continue to ignore violation of ceasefire terms with various insurgent groups and not go all out to eliminate them. If the insurgency can be defeated in Tripura and Sri Lanka, why can we not do the same in Assam, Manipur and Nagaland?

Conclusion

In the Indian political system, the leader's interest comes first, the party interest comes second and national interest comes last always and every time. We seem to be a country of self-seeking "Baniyas" or businessmen for whom national pride and sovereignty has no meaning whatsoever. I do not know how long we will last as an independent nation without being broken up.

Epilogue

I am not really afraid of the Chinese Dragon. I acknowledge that China is a much bigger economic and military power than India. I acknowledge that China has successfully used India "big brother" bogey and economic and military aid to wean away India's neighbours into its sphere of influence. I recognize the possibility of our neighbours siding with China in a future conflict. I acknowledge that Eastern Command and Arunachal Pradesh are inadequately defended. But China has its own problems of unrest in Tibet and Xinjiang Provinces and the possibility of class war between the urban rich and the rural poor, millions of whom have been rendered jobless as China's exports fell and factories closed. It is also inconceivable that the world would continue to allow cheap imports from China ruin their economies. Chinese soldiers are not supermen. They have seen far less action than Indian Army has. I have full faith in the fighting abilities of the Indian jawans and young officers. They have fought numerically superior, better equipped armies to the last man, last round at the citadel of Skardu, the snowbound slopes of Rezang La, at the untenable defences at the bridges on Namka Chu and the isolated defences of Walong. They have captured Haji Pir, Tiger Hill, and Tololing to name a few.

I am afraid of the Indian political system where the mission of the party in power is not to make India a strong, vibrant country, but to engage in compulsive populism to ensure victory in the next elections, spending billions of Rupees on schemes like NREGA which is destroying rural work culture, ruining agriculture and taking corruption to unprecedented levels. The parties in power are providing free electricity to villages, slums and making electricity production and distribution economically unviable, providing subsidized petroleum products at the cost of the nationalized oil producing and distributing companies and taking them to the verge of collapse or foreign takeover. Thus, we do not have money to fill vacancies in the police, paramilitary forces, of teachers, health workers and even judges. We do not have money to increase power generation, to provide drinking water or improve infrastructure. We do not have the political will to establish the rule of law, to carry out police reforms, to stop misuse of VIP privileges, get MPs and MLAs, government departments and bureaucrats to pay their electricity and telephone bills and to vacate government accommodation when they are no longer authorized to occupy them. We do not have the will to make government servants and ministers accountable for their acts of omissions and commissions. Can such a political system ever produce a strong India? I pine for a benevolent dictator who will sweep out the ills which plague our political system and reintroduce constitutional propriety, rule of law, accountability in government departments and provide safety and security to the man on the street.

I am afraid of the timidity of our political leadership. Small countries like Iran, North Korea, Serbia, Sri Lanka, Syria, Venezuela, Hezbolla and even Hamas can defy American dictates. But our leaders, leaders of a country of over one billion people which has the fourth largest armed forces in the world and the fifth largest economy, seem to shiver at the thought of invoking American displeasure. Pakistan can say that there can be no permanent peace with India unless Kashmir issue is solved but India cannot say that there will not be any bilateral relations between India and Pakistan unless Pakistan stops its soil from being used for terrorists attacks on India. If Vajpayee had the courage of Lal Bahadur Shastri, he would have ordered the Indian Army not only to recapture all heights captured by Pakistanis at Kargil including Pt. 3535 but also Skardu, the base through which all the military actions in the sector take place. It would have helped the souls of the soldiers who defended Skardu and were lined up and shot after surrendering when their ammunition ran out and their wives and daughters who were raped, rest in peace. If he had an iota of feeling for the Indian jawans, he would have filed war crimes charges against Pakistan for the brutal torture, dismembering and killing of Lieutenant Kalia and the five jawans who were captured by the enemy on the first day of the Kargil war. I am ashamed to hear our Prime Minister say that "war is not an option". War is very much an option of state policy. It has been so for centuries and will continue to be so. India must always be ready for it. It is the duty of our political leaders to defend our country and our economic sovereignty and interest, to uphold the constitution and rule of law. If they are incapable of doing so, let them resign. I pine for a strong leader who is a nationalist like Subhash Chandra Bose (Netaji), Lal Bahadur Shastri, Mrs. Indira Gandhi or President Rajapakshe of Sri Lanka who can ignore external and internal pressures from vested interests and do what is best for the country.

I am afraid of our senior military leadership. For years, military planning has been based on the assumption, "There will be no war and if there is war, I will not be there to fight it". Every senior commander, who has ever disagreed with the threat perception of his senior or has stated that the resources allotted to him are inadequate for the task allotted, has been passed over for promotion. Promotions are not made in a transparent manner. Extreme data which do not conform to established trends are rejected in any statistical analysis. But rejections and promotions in the defence forces are usually based on the lowest marks in annual confidential reports (usually a result of a professional disagreement or an ego clash with a superior) or sudden unexplained jump in marks (usually a result of favouritism or nepotism). The situation is so bad that almost every senior officer who is passed over for promotion files a statutory complaint or goes to court claiming injustice. With almost the entire senior hierarchy of the armed forces focused on promoting their careers, where is the time for monitoring operational preparedness, training, morale of troops (over a 150 soldiers commit suicide every year) and other frivolous issues. Who cares if there is a shortage of snow mobiles in Siachin, bulletproof vests in insurgency areas or shortage of young officers? (The problem of shortage of young officers is not new. It was there in 1990, it is still there twenty years later in 2009 and it will continue. If the Army was keen to solve it, it would have. But they are not. If any one wants the solution, I have it.) Who cares if a MiG 21 or 27 goes down and kills the pilot? I pine for military leaders like General Jayant Chowdhury, Air Marshal Engineer, General L.P. Sen, General Harbaksh Singh, General Sam Manekshaw, General P.S. Bhagat and General Sardeshpande whose impeccable professional abilities, integrity, leadership qualities and values inspired thousands of their followers to give their best.

I am afraid of India's pacifist intellectuals like Praful Bidwai who give more importance to creating goodwill than military power as an instrument of state policy. I do not know if their articles are sponsored by countries and lobbies who do not want to see a strong and sovereign India. Nehru tried to cultivate goodwill with China. Short of handing over Dalai Lama and conceding Arunachal, he did everything. We know the results. Vajpayee tried to create goodwill with Pakistan. He started people to people contacts, introduced bus and train services and encouraged trade. The result was easier inflow of ISI agents, easier inflow of drugs and weapons, more terrorist attacks on India and Pakistani occupation of Kargil. He even invited Musharraf only to be rebuffed at the Agra summit. The media is still queuing up for inviting Musharraf for interviews. These pacifists are always confusing the people and lulling them into complacency. India can survive a hundred years of hostility with Pakistan more comfortably than Pakistan can. So, there is no need to submit to Pakistani threats and give away Kashmir or accept terrorism. Terrorist bases in POK must be destroyed. Let Pakistan go to war if it chooses to. It has done that four times and achieved nothing. It can never defeat India.

I am afraid that India's luck in armed conflicts with its neighbours may not last. Pakistan failed to grab Kashmir in 1947, not because India anticipated the attack and was ready to defend Kashmir. They failed because they stopped to loot and rape Baramula and because of the sacrifices of a few companies of Jammu and Kashmir State Army who held out long enough for Indian Army reinforcements to arrive and stop the enemy. India did not survive the Chinese attacks in 1962, because of its ability to defend itself. It had, for all purposes, surrendered Arunachal Pradesh along with the the part of Assam which lay on the north bank of the Bramhaputra River when China decided to declare ceasefire and withdrew to the positions from where they had started. Pakistan failed to breakout of the bridgehead it had established at Khemkaran opposite Kasur (Pakistan) during the 1965 Indo-Pak War because an accidental flooding bogged down the Pakistani tanks and an isolated Indian section, the only one that had not fled in face of the Pakistani assault, killed the Pakistani armored brigade commander in a freak ambush and held up the breakout by a day. This allowed the Indian Army to plug the gaps in defenses and finally prevail at the battle of Assal Uttar. Pakistan failed to capture Jaisalmer during 1971 Indo-Pak War with an armored thrust, because the Pakistani thrust lost their way and were held up by the a valiant infantry company only to be picked up by the Indian Air Force in the morning and destroyed from the air. I pray that India will not have to depend on luck or the hand of God to save it from disaster during the next war.

Pacifists have not learned the lessons from history. The Mauryan Empire reached its peak during the rule of Ashoka the Great. Ashoka became a pacifist after the Battle of Kalinga in 263 BCE and neglected military matters. After Ashoka died in 232 BCE, the Mauryan Empire, which stretched from Afghanistan to the Godavari River, collapsed within fifty years. Nehru was a pacifist. He led India to its most humiliating military defeat since independence. War is very much an option for nations that value their sovereignty and independence, even if it is the option of last resort. From the time of Sun Tzu

(500 BCE), it is recognized that the only pragmatic and prudent approach to threat perception and defence preparedness is to go by the capability and not the intention of our possible adversaries. Intentions can change with a change of government or a head of state. And in today's violent and volatile world, governments and intentions can change overnight. But it takes tens of years and trillions of Rupees to build a credible military deterrence that will discourage our neighbours from military misadventures.

May God save India, not only from its enemies but also from its pacifists and political leaders.

Bibliography

Part 1 - Background

Chapter 1: Historical Relations

www.en.wikipedia.org

Chapter 2: Conflicts of Interest

"India and China Row Over Border", *BBC News*, 14 November 2006.

"UK Recognizes China's Direct Rule over Tibet" by Richard Spencer, *The Daily Telegraph*, 5 November 2008.

www.in.wokipedia.org

Part 2 - Military Reasons for Concern

Chapter 3: China's Military Might

U.S. Department of Defense, "Military Power of the People's Republic of China 2007."

Congressional Research Service, "China Naval Modernization: Implications for U.S. Navy Capabilities."

Centre for Strategic and International Studies

www.globalsecurity.org/china

www.asianhistory.about.com

The Military Balance—International Institute for Strategic Studies

www. Globalfirepower.com

Roy, Bhaskar, China's Military Budget—Should India be Concerned?

Chapter 4: China Relations with Pakistan

"New Developments in Pakistan-China Relations" by Tanvir Ahmad Khan, *Arab News*, 6 August 2007.

Singh, Dr. Swaran, "Pakistan-China Defence Cooperation", May 1996.

Kuppuswamy, C.S., "China-Pakistan-Myanmar: The Triangular Relationship Needs Careful Watch".

"Chinese Military Supplies to Pakistan", News Behind the News, January 14, 2002.

Ramana, Siddharth, "China-Pakistan: An Unholy Nuclear Alliance", December 4, 2008.

Parthasarathy G., "Make No Mistake", *Times of India*, January 5, 2009.

——. "The May Mystery", *Times of India*, January 7, 2009.

Chapter 5: China's Relations with Bangladesh

www.earthtimes.com

www.anglefire.com

Kapila, Dr. Subhash, "Bangladesh-China Defence Cooperation Agreement's Strategic implications: *An Analysis*" in Nepram, B., *South Asia's Fractured Frontiers*, 2002.

www.southasiaanalysis.org

www.iceweb2.loc.gov

www.banglapedia.search.com

www.virtualbangladesh.com

Sen, Sumit, "Bangladesh Building Missile Arsenal" *TNN*, 12 September 2008.

Chapter 6: China's Relations with Sri Lanka

www.wikipedia.org – Sri Lankan Army

www.Tamilnation.org

Intelligence reports of Merchyhurst Institute of Intelligence Studies:

China's Oil Quest Across India's Cauvery Basin, SAAG Paper No. 2181, B. Raman, 26 March, 2007.

Chapter 7: China's Relations with Myanmar

www.southasiaanalysis.org/paper5

www.wikipedia.org

Chapter 8: China' Relations with Nepal

www.newstrackindia.com

www.fmprc.gov.cn
www.china.org.cn
www.country-data.com

Chapter 9: China's Build-up in Tibet

www.amnestyusa.org
www.indiadefensereview.com
www.shadowforeignpolicy.com
Kanwa Defense Review, monthly published from Toronto.
www.globalsecurity.org

Chapter 10: India's Military Problems

www.globalsecurity.org
www.Fas.org/nuke/guide/pakistan/missile
www.nti.org
En.wikipedia.org/wiki/sino-india_war
En.wikipedia.org?wiki/Indo-Pak_war
www.bharat-rakshak.com/landforces/army/1962war

Part 3 - Other Reasons for Concern

Chapter 11: Economic Reasons for Concern

en.wikipedia.org
www.carthtimes.org
The Economist
www.Chinadaily.com
Indiaenews.com
Domain-b.com

Chapter 12: Political Reasons for Concern

Epilogue

Index